MINDFUL MAZES
ADULT COLORING BOOK

Marty Noble's

mandalas

Racehorse Publishing books may be purchased in bulk at special discounts for sales promotion, corporate gifts, fund-raising, or educational purposes. Special editions can also be created to specifications. For details, contact the Special Sales Department, Skyhorse Publishing, 307 West 36th Street, 11th Floor, New York, NY 10018 or info@skyhorsepublishing.com.

Racehorse Publishing™ is a pending trademark of Skyhorse Publishing, Inc.®, a Delaware corporation.

Visit our website at www.skyhorsepublishing.com.

10 9 8 7 6 5 4

Cover design by Brian Peterson
Cover illustration by Marty Noble

ISBN: 978-1-944686-20-8

Printed in the United States of America

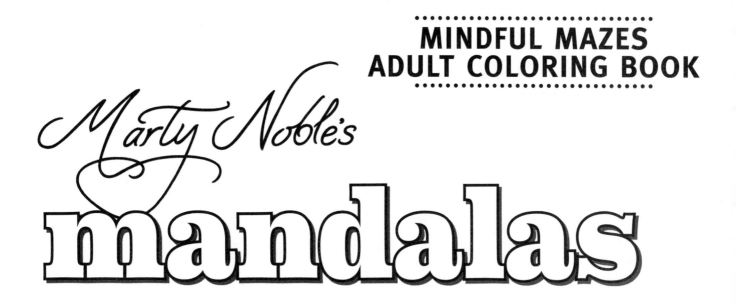

Marty Noble's
mandalas

**48 Engaging Mazes That Will
Challenge Your Creativity and Wisdom!**

MARTY NOBLE

Racehorse Publishing

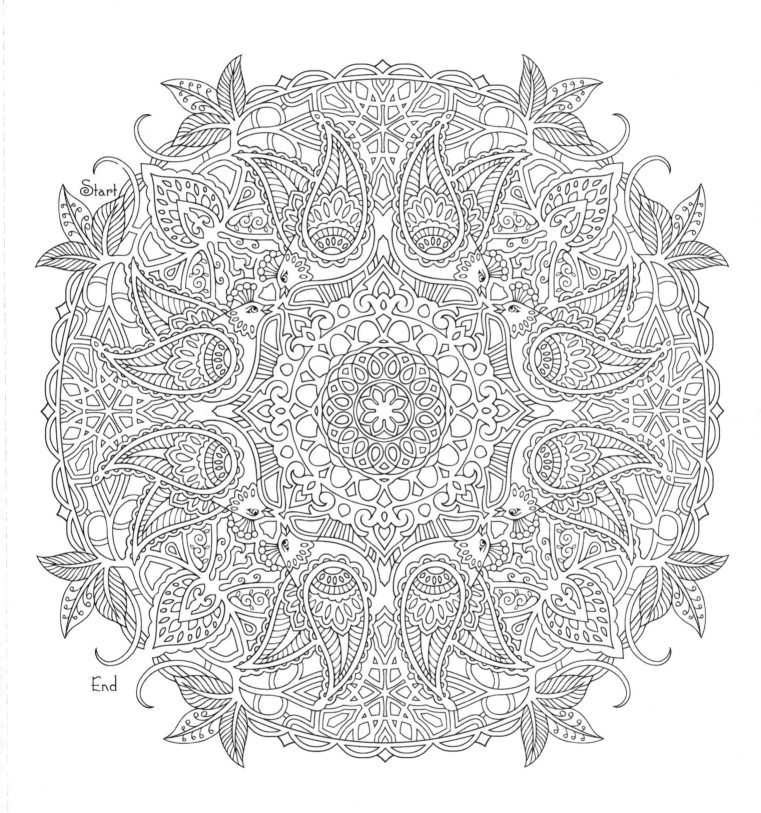

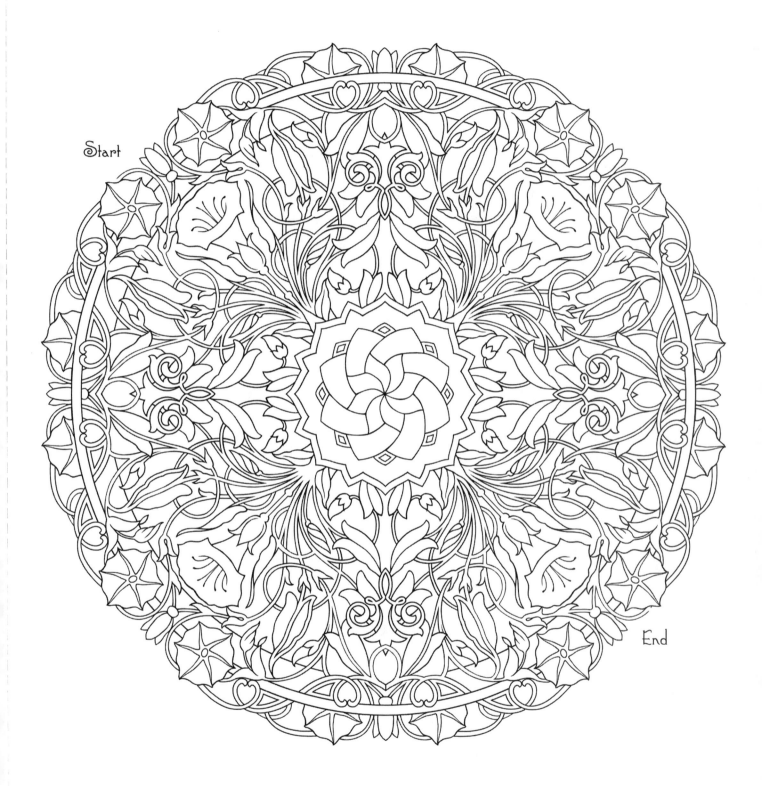

Start

End

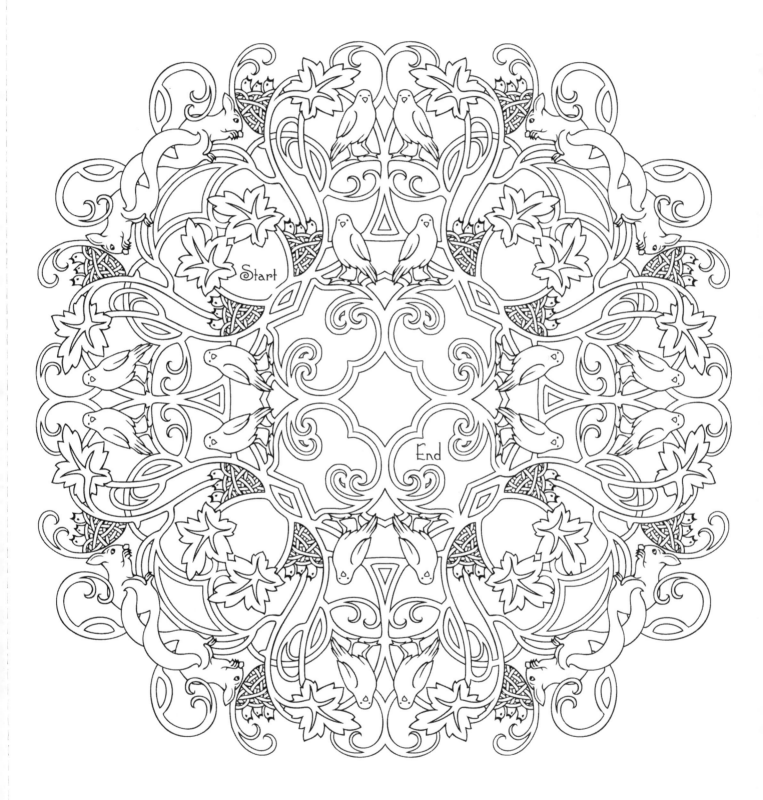

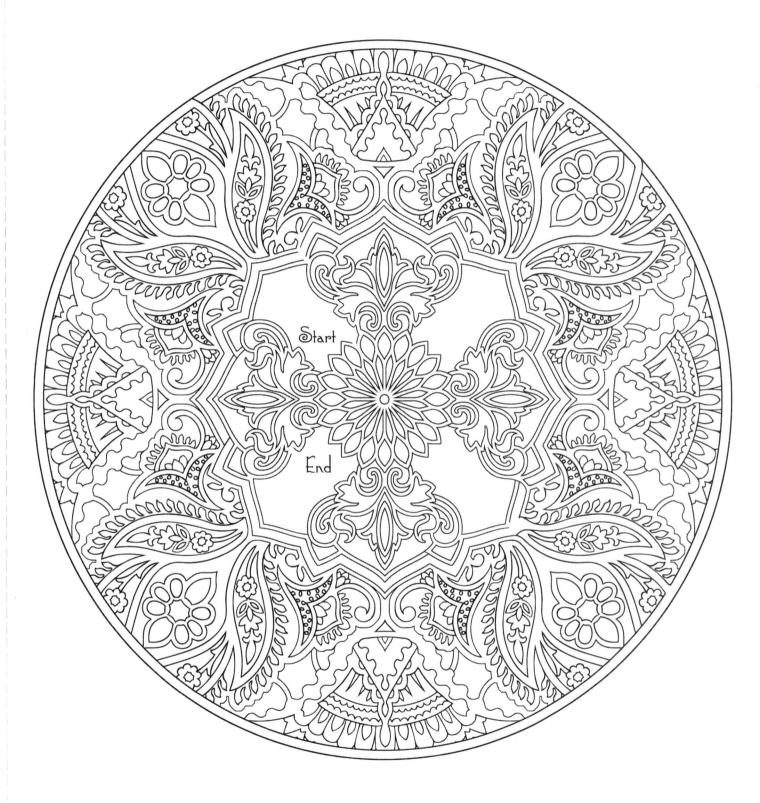

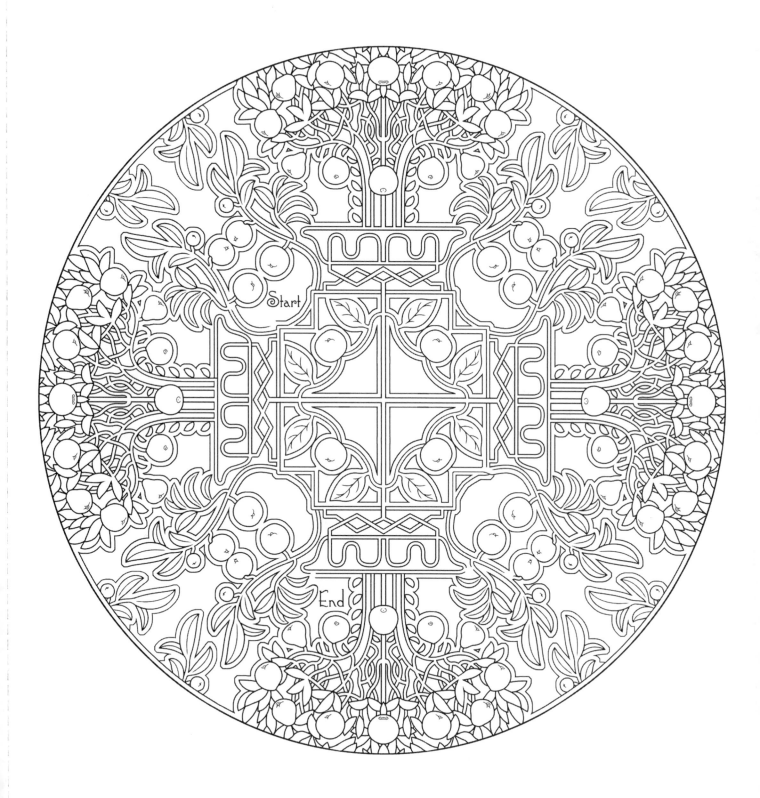

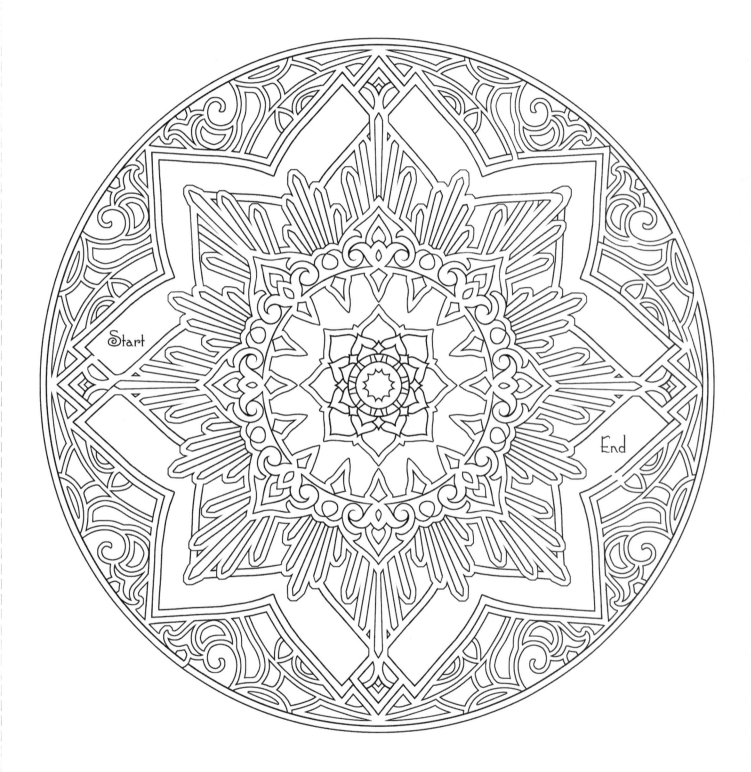

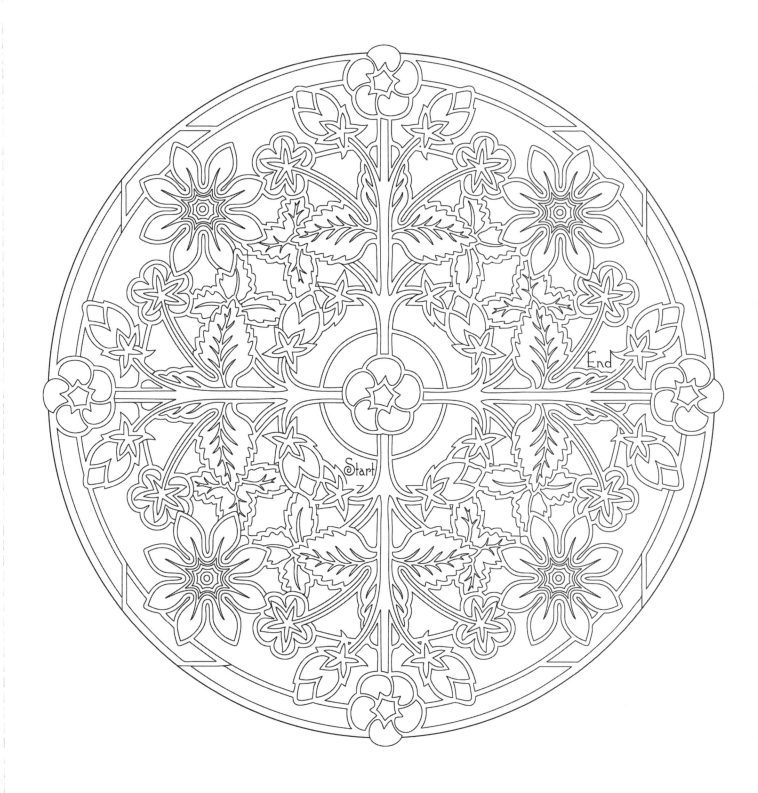

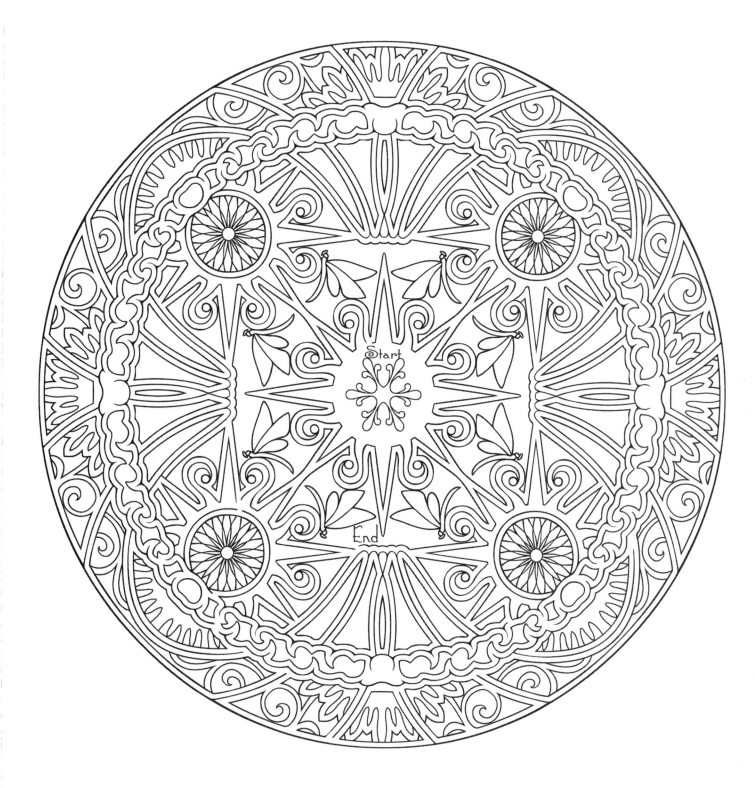

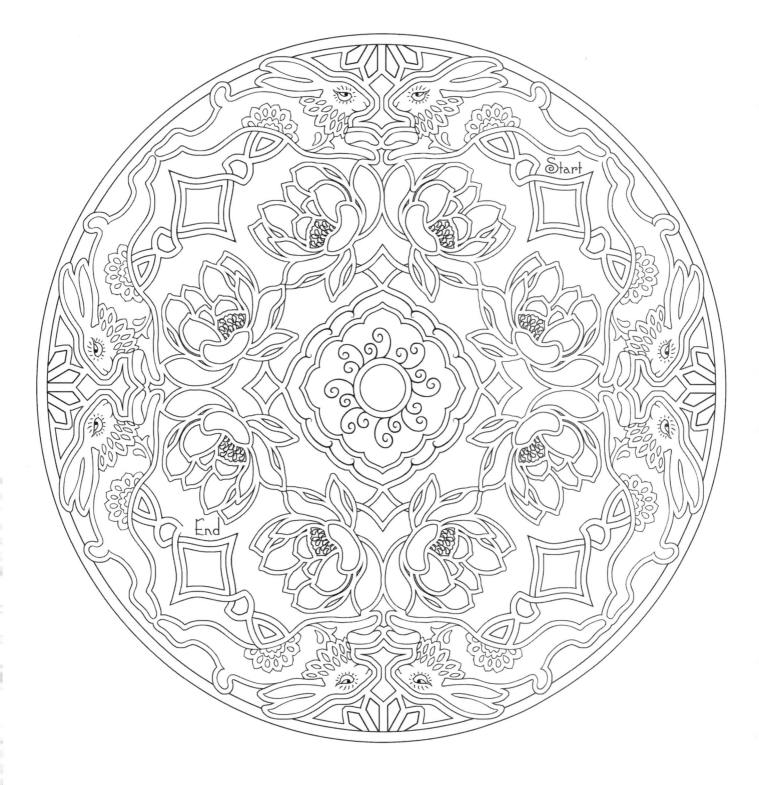

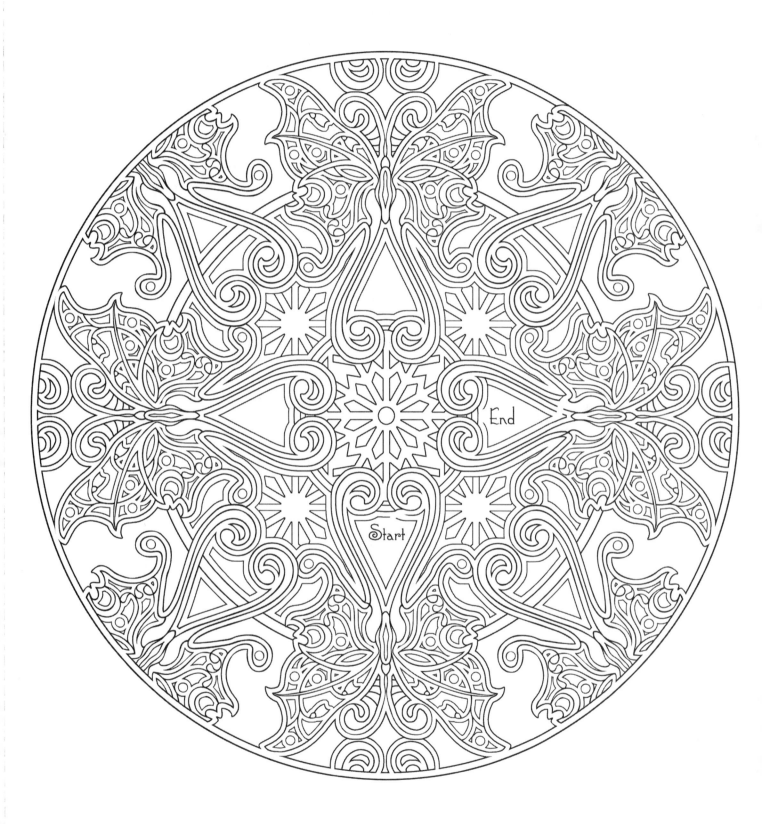

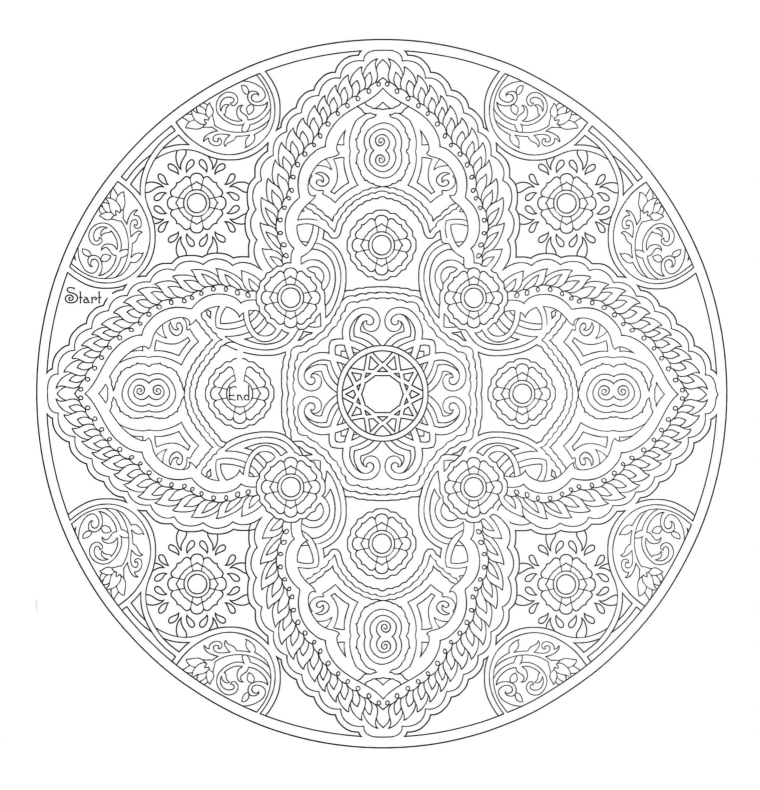

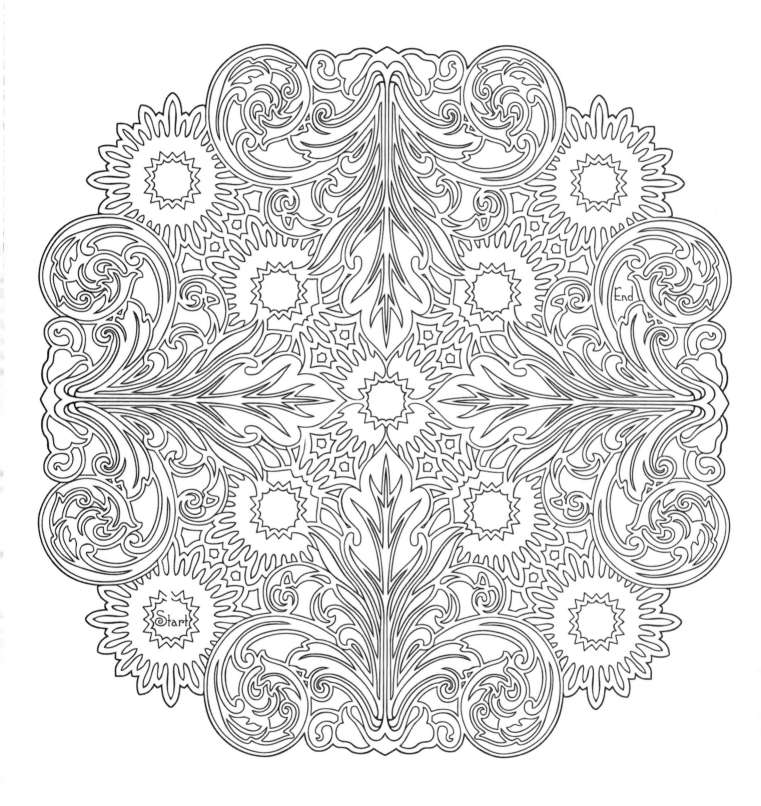

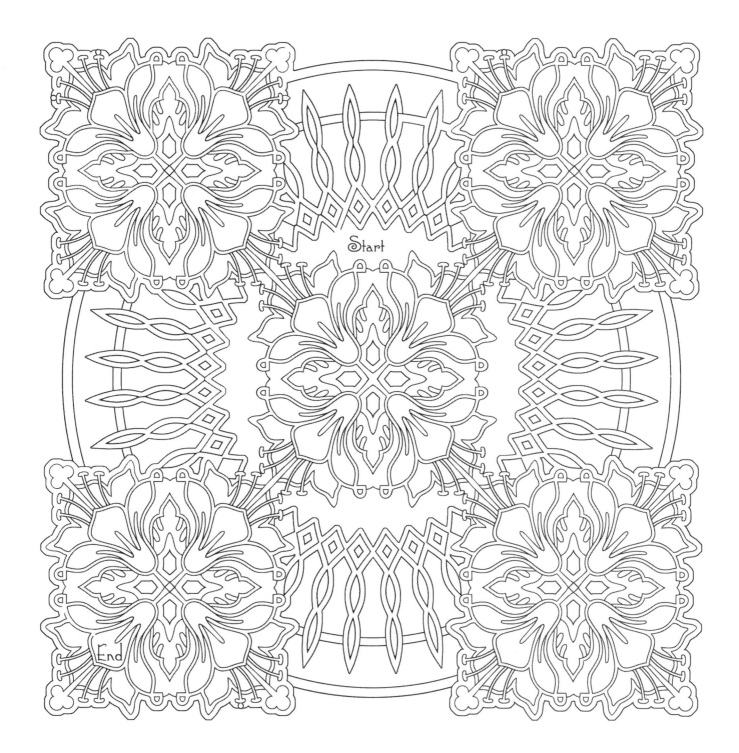

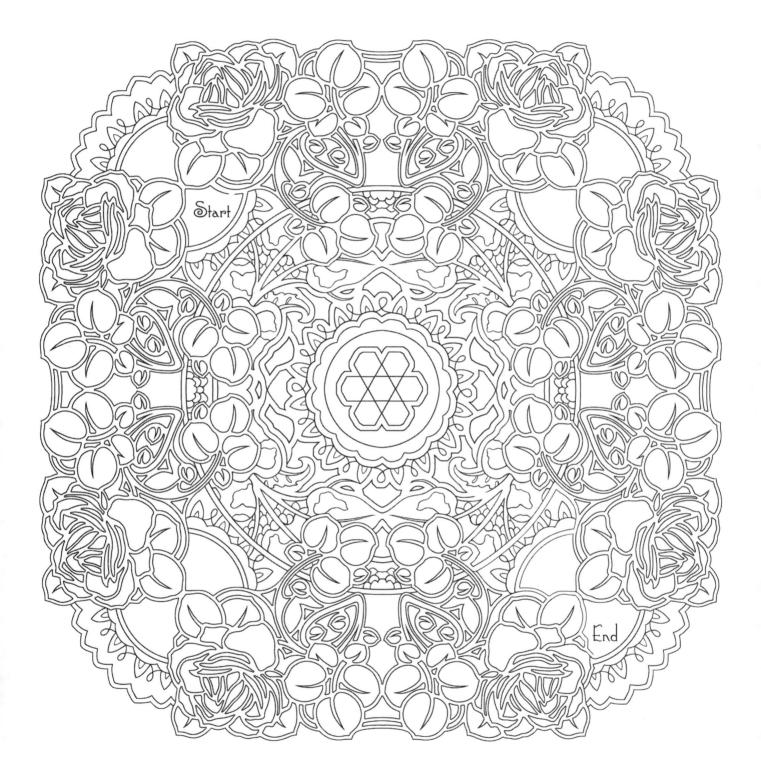

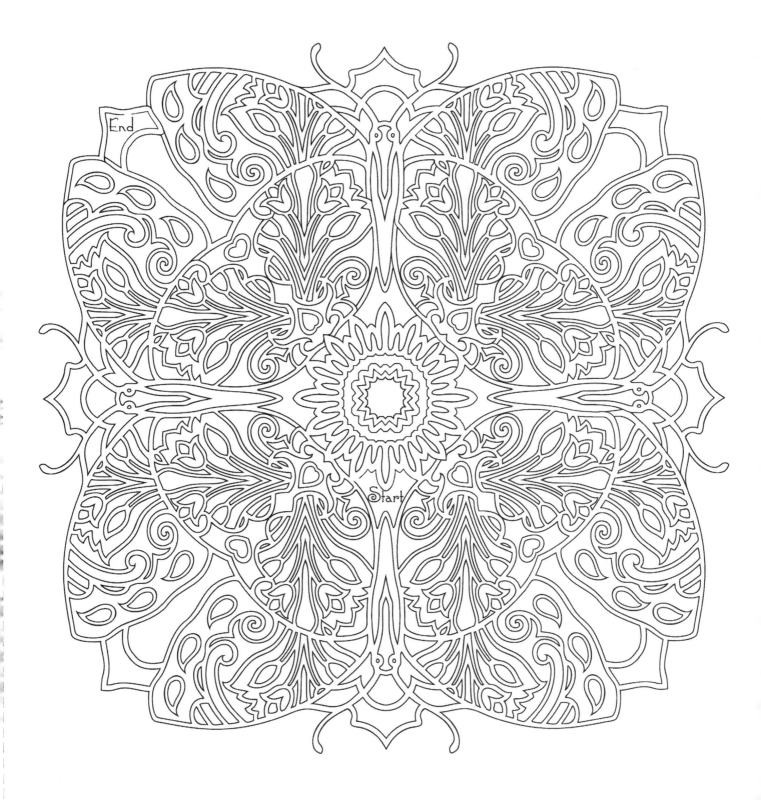

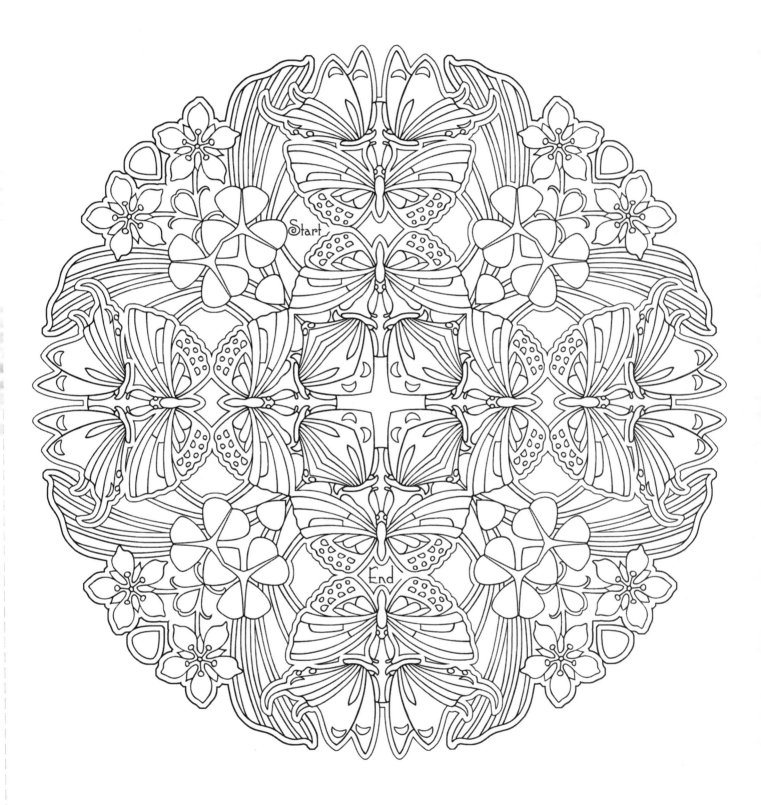

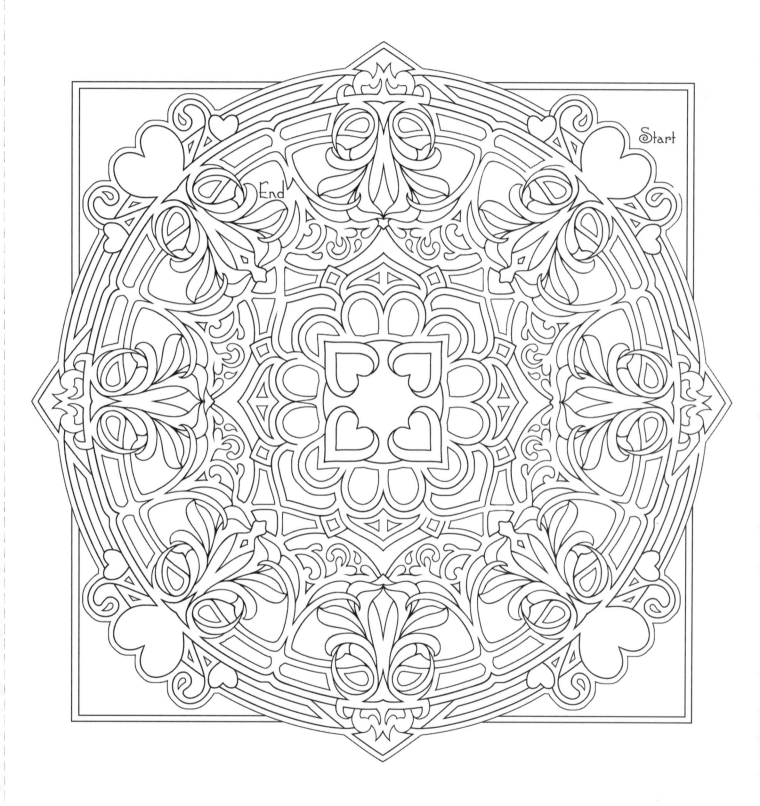

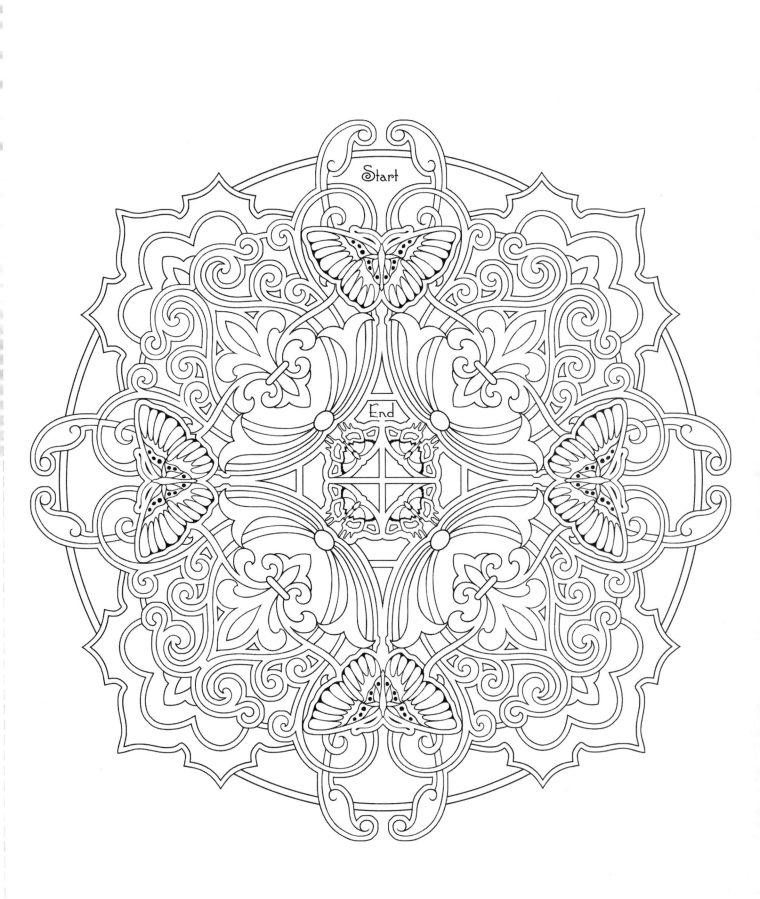

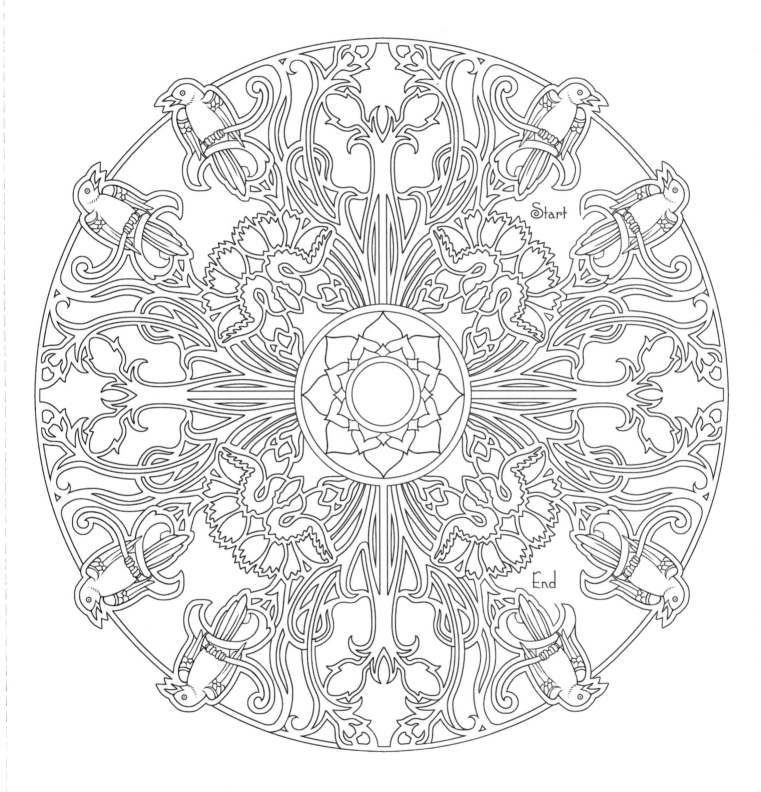

Start

End

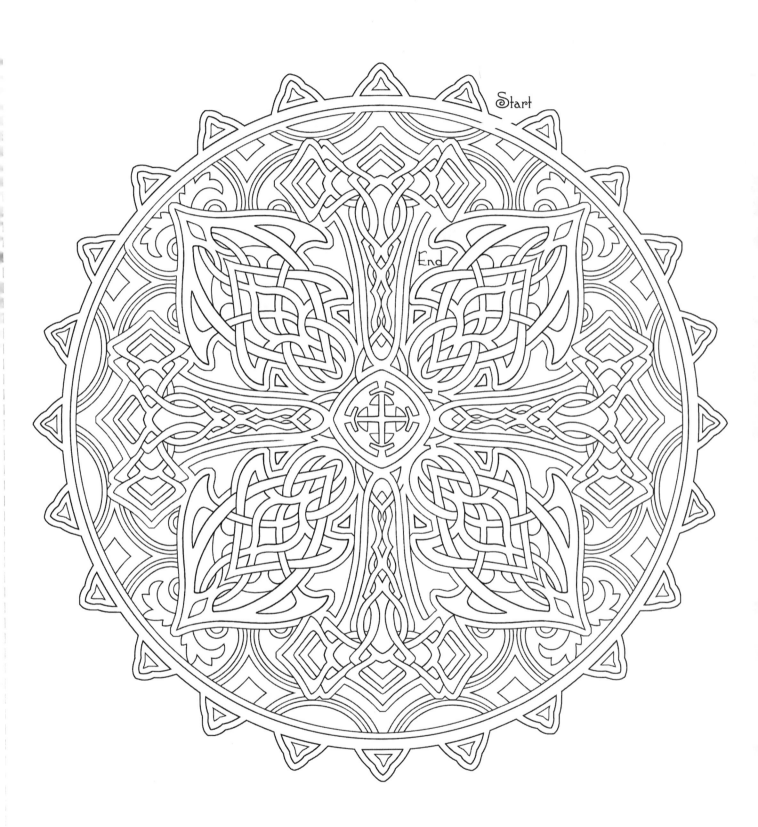

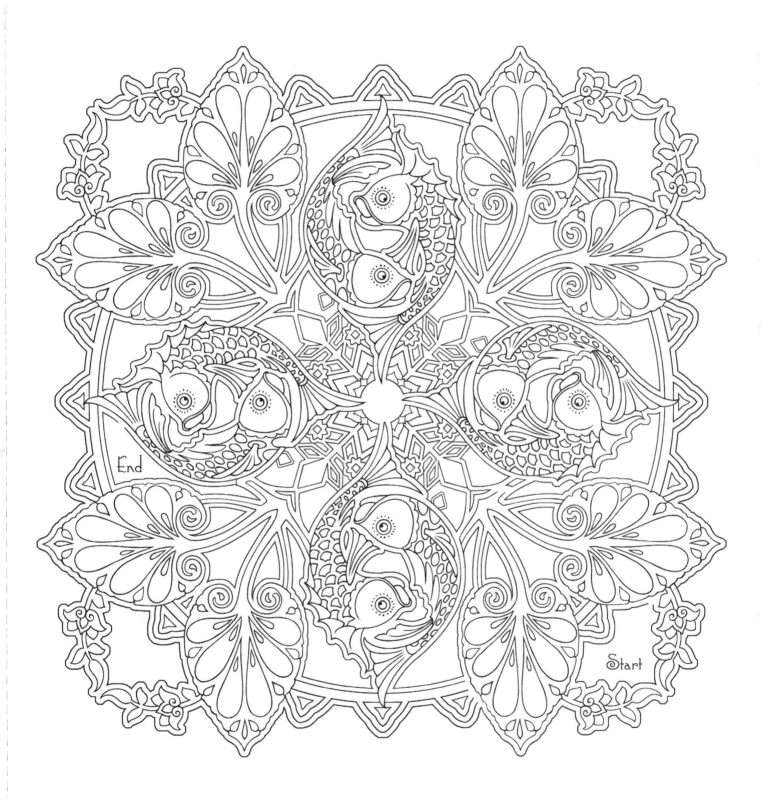

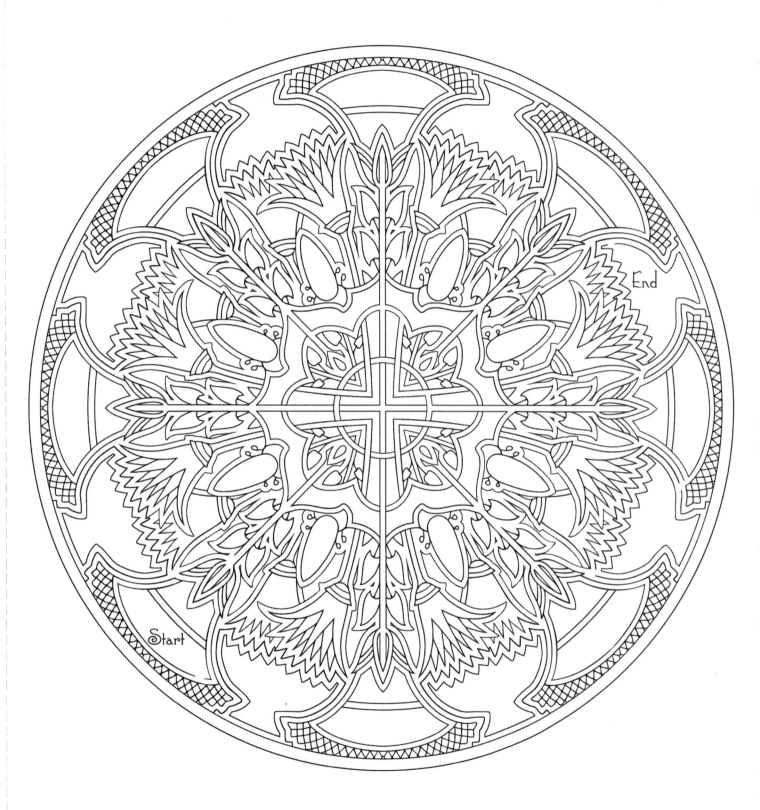

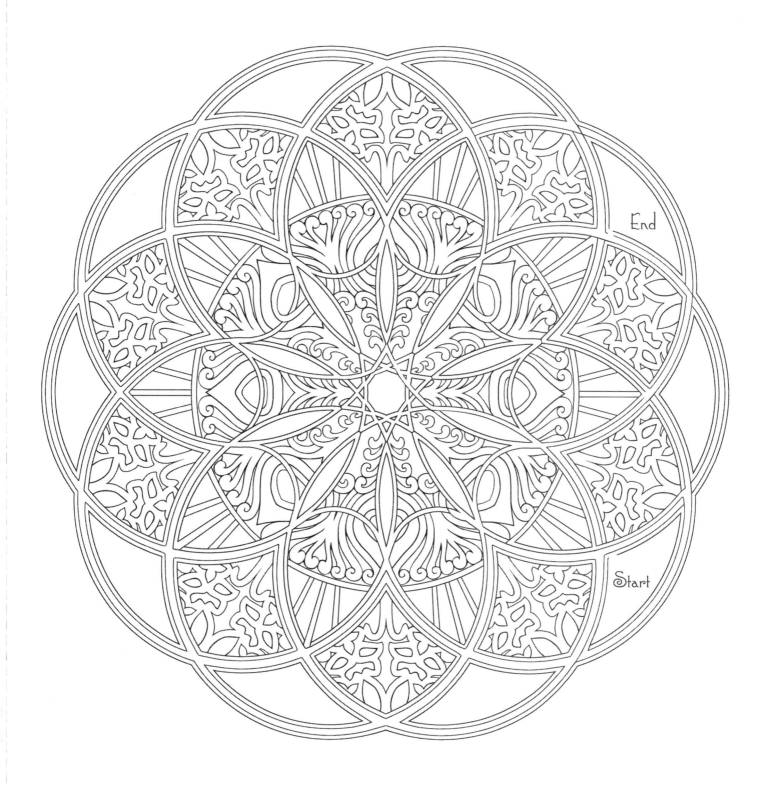
End

Start

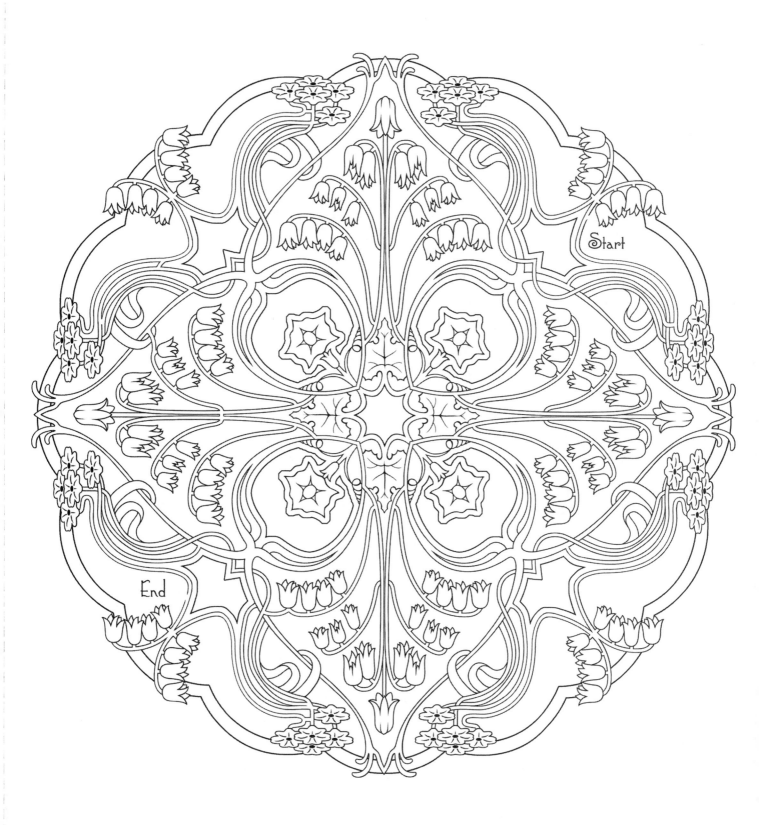

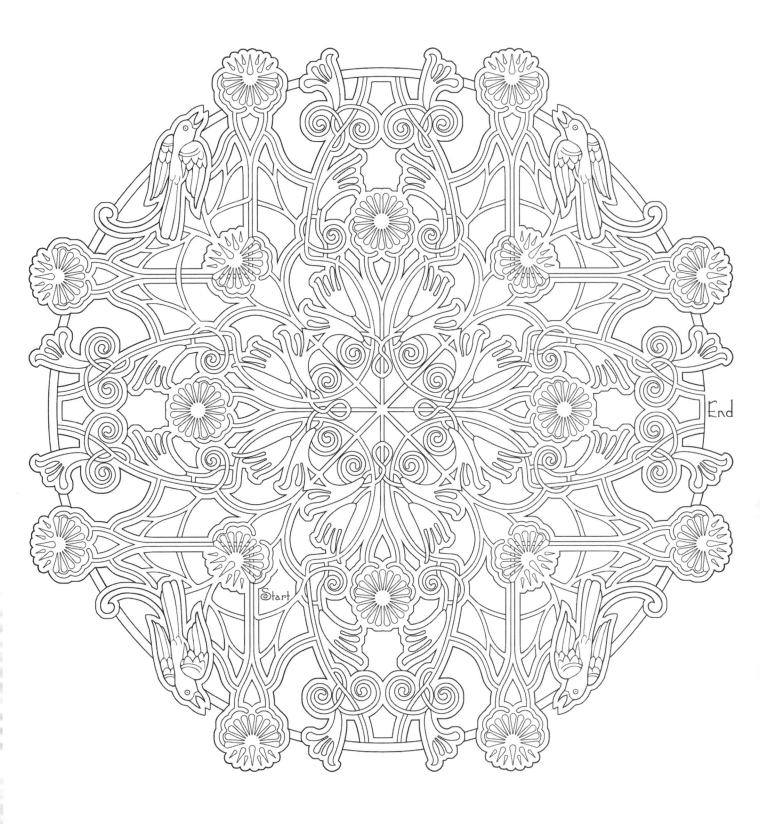

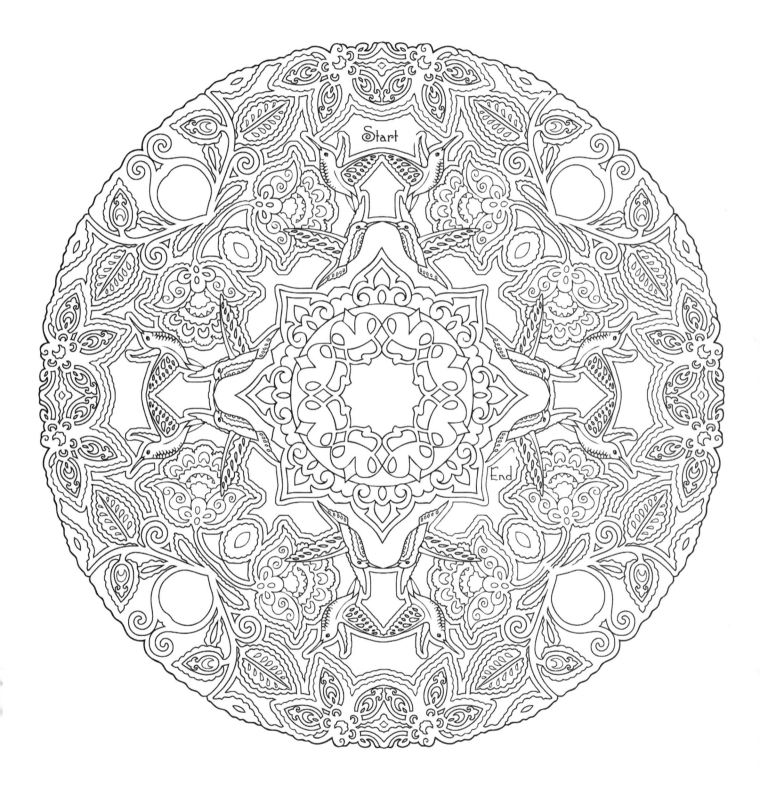

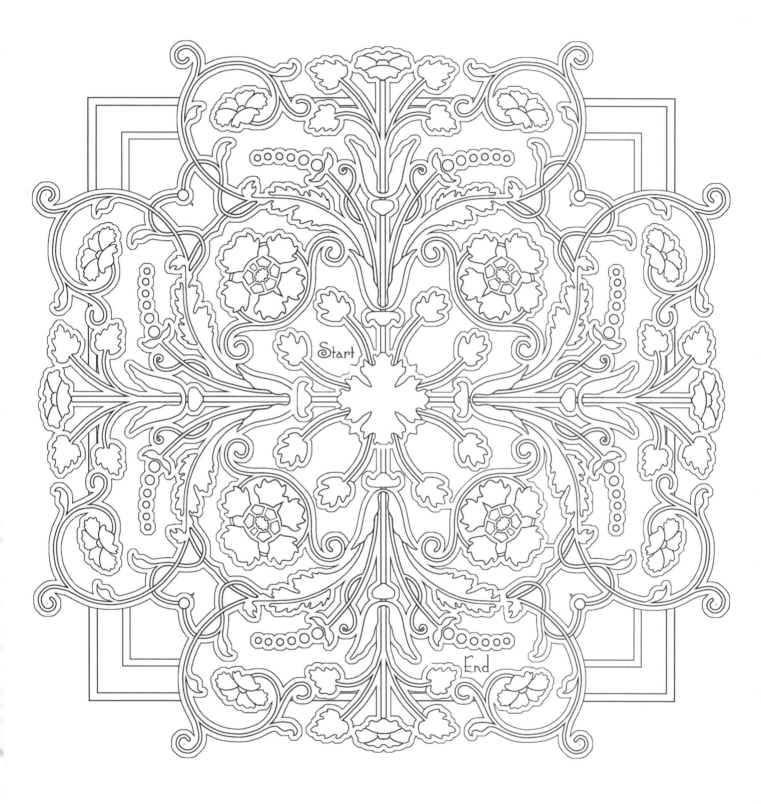

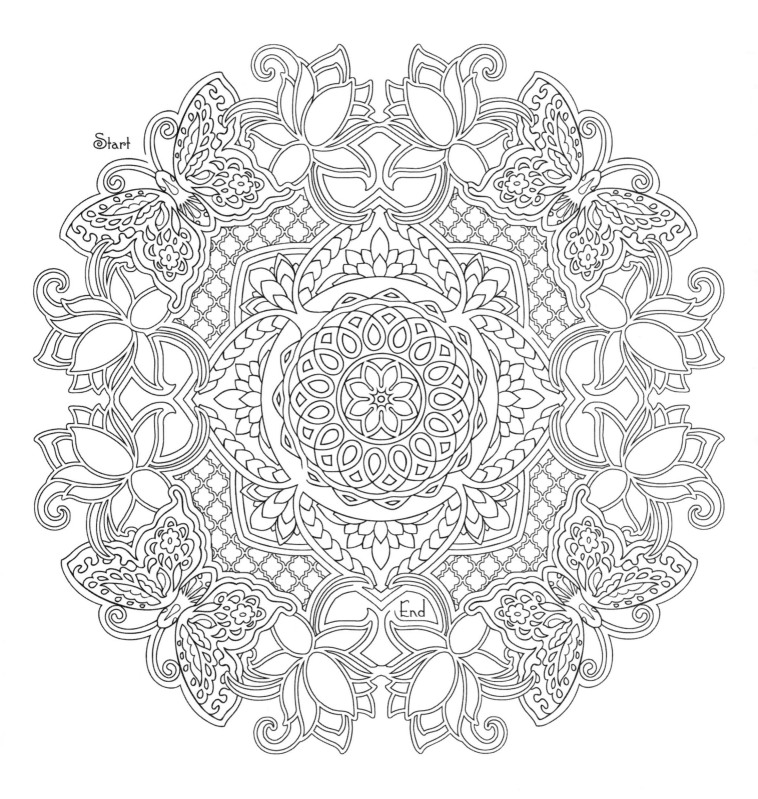

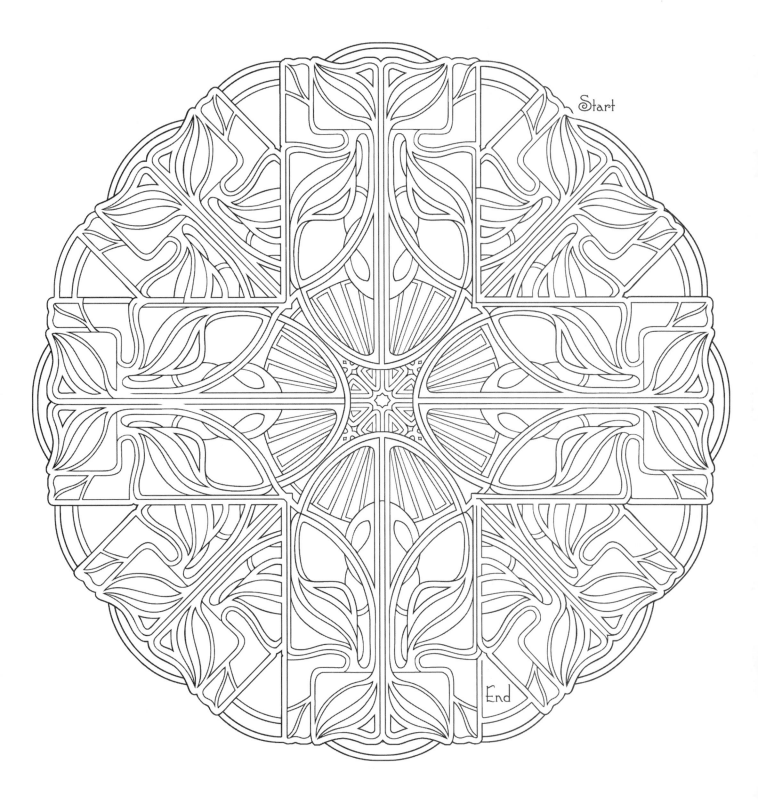

Start

End

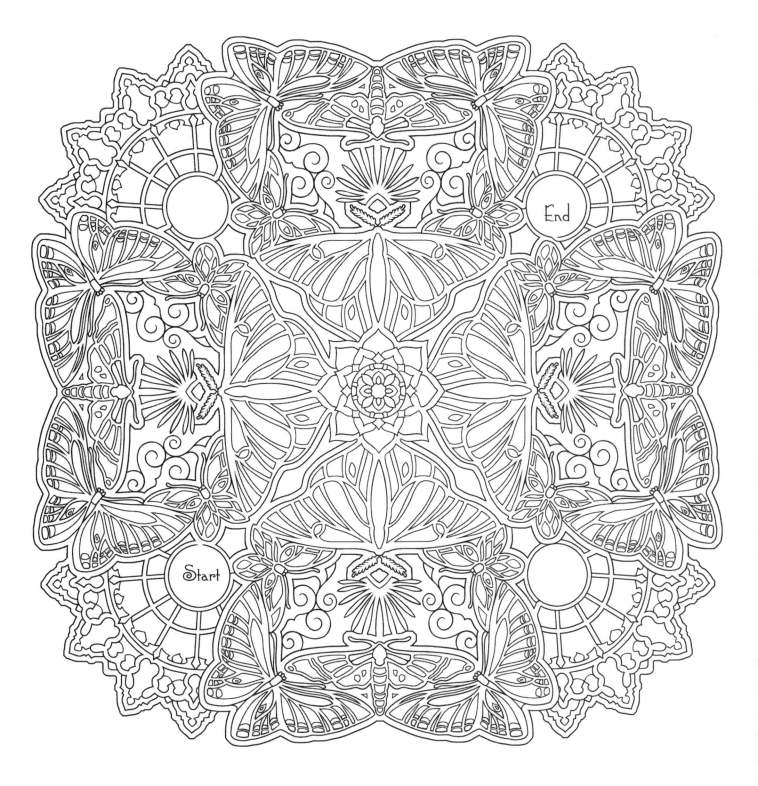

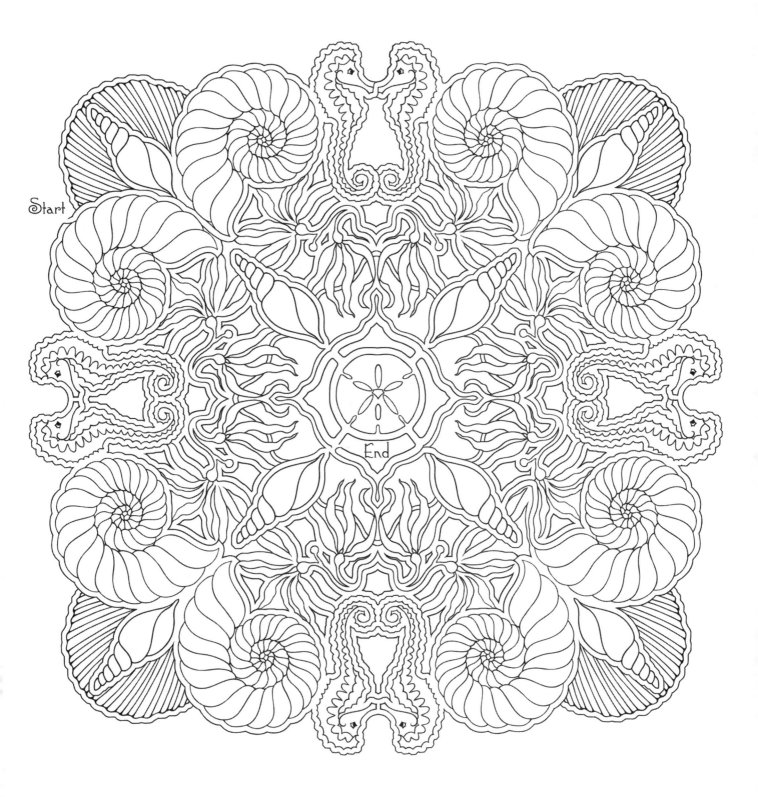
Start

End

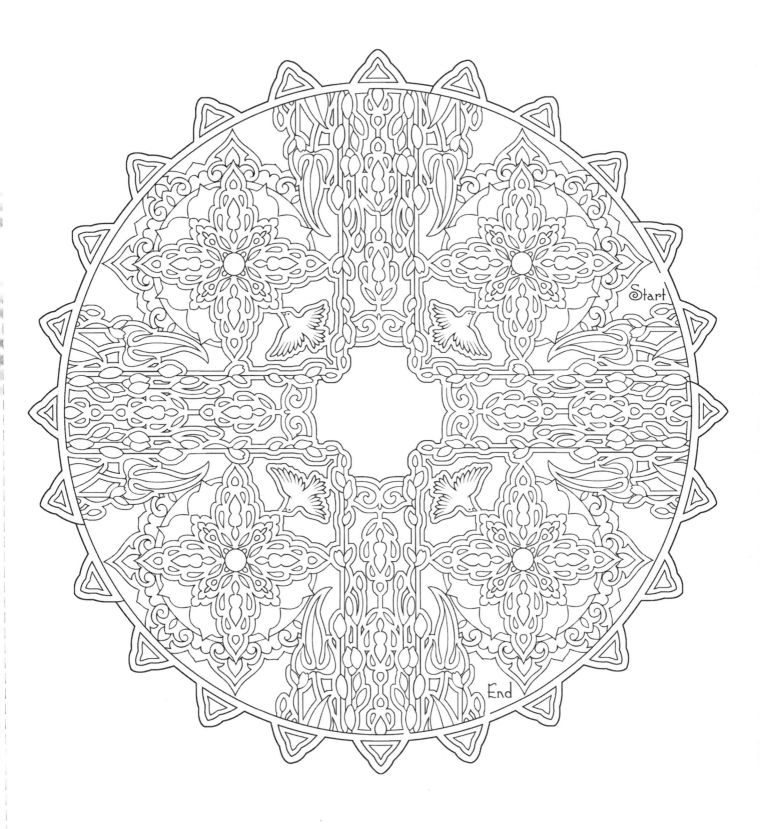

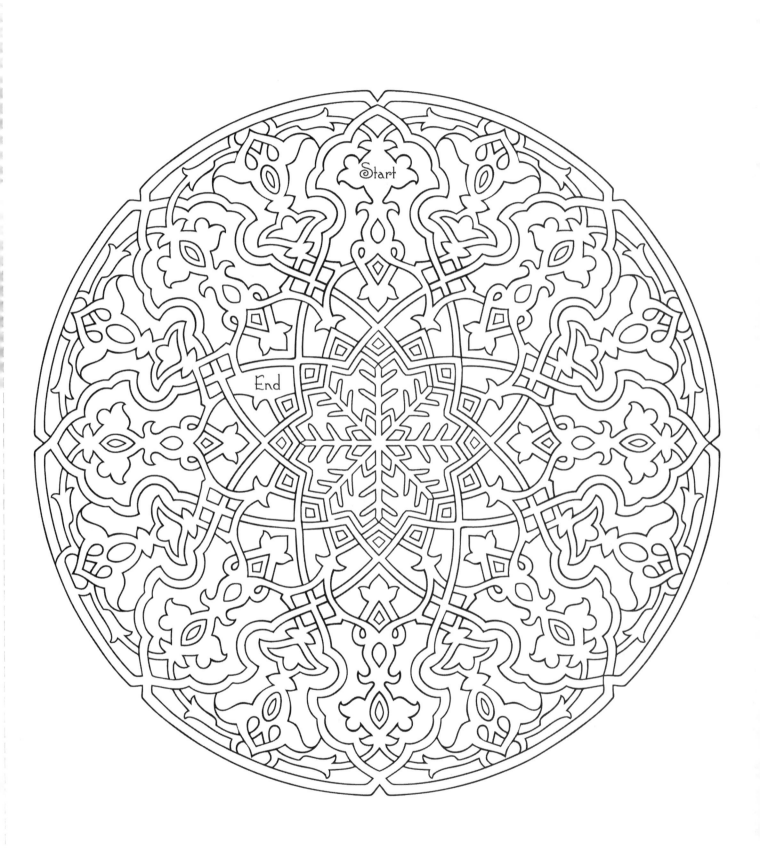

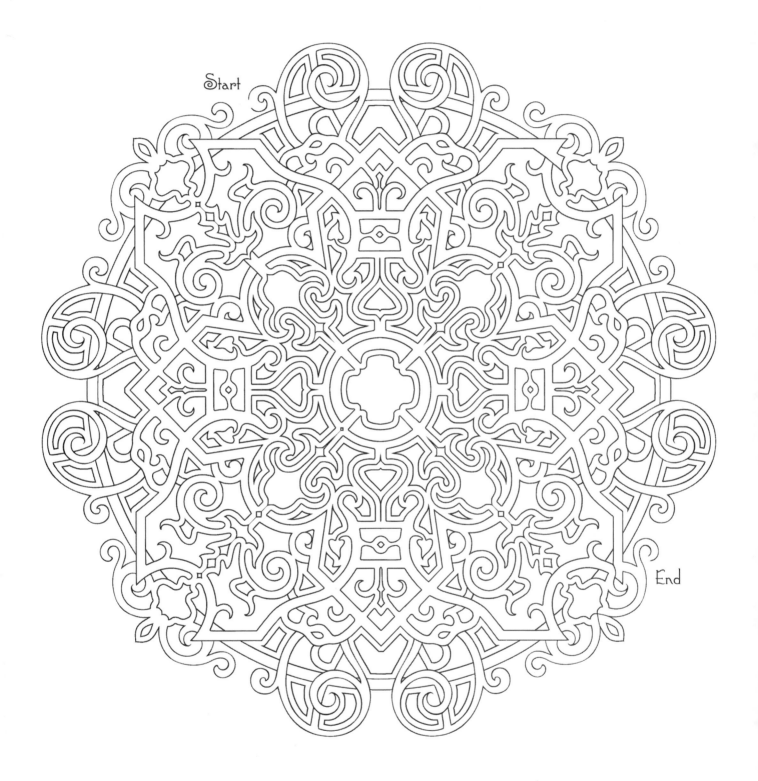

Start

End

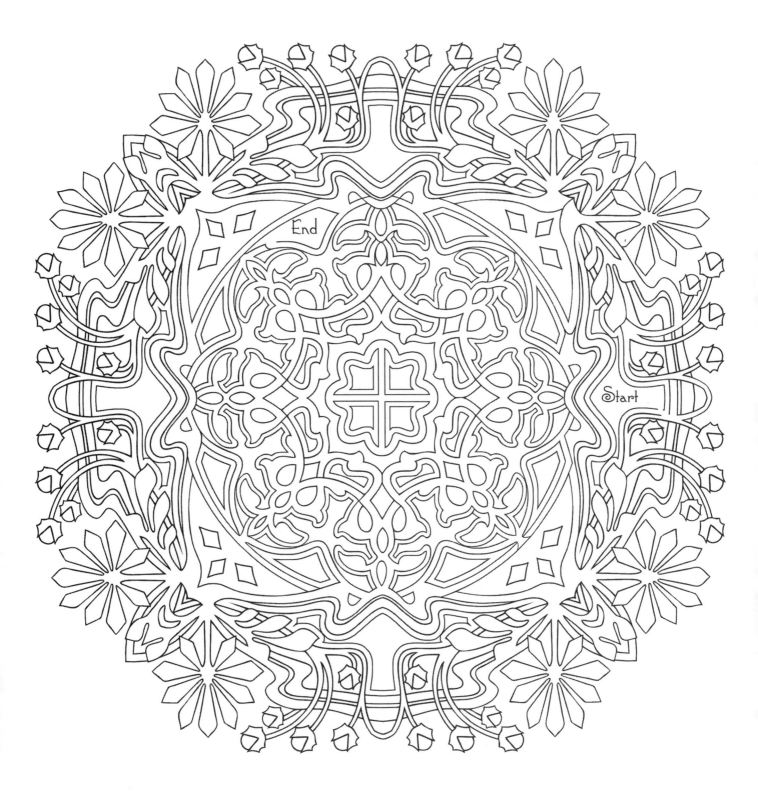

Start   End

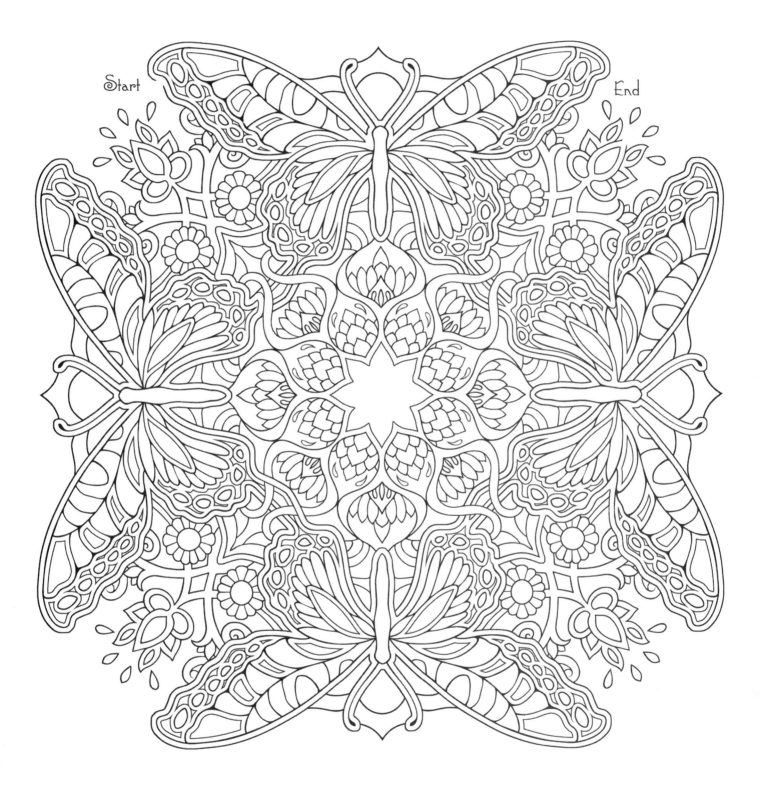

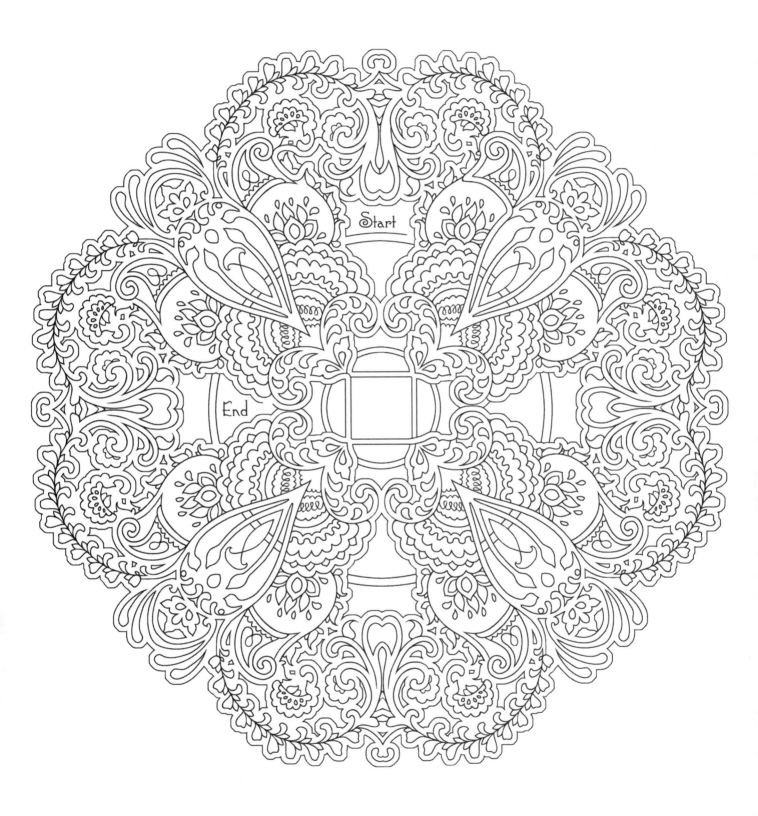

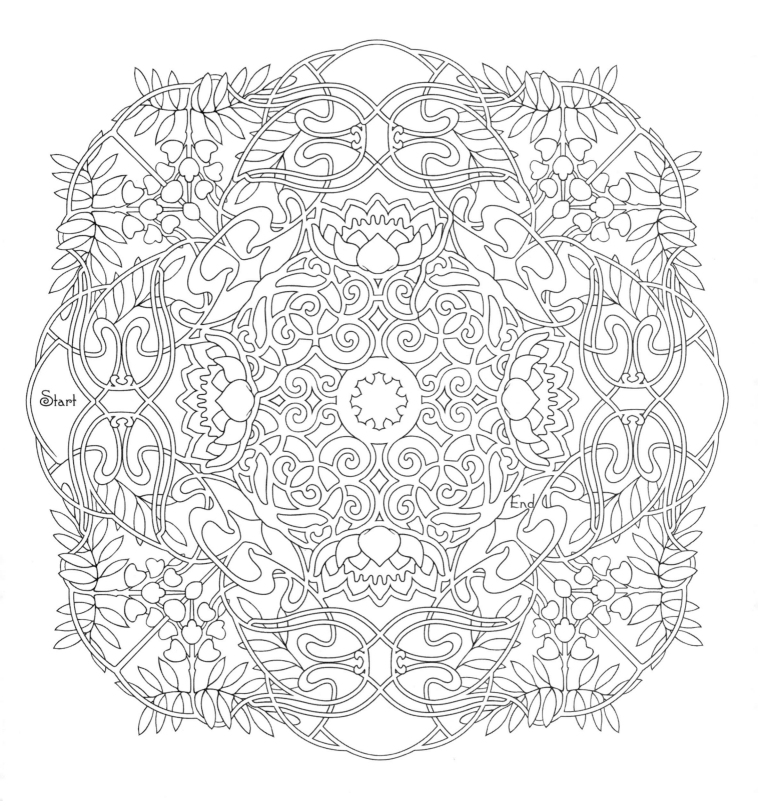

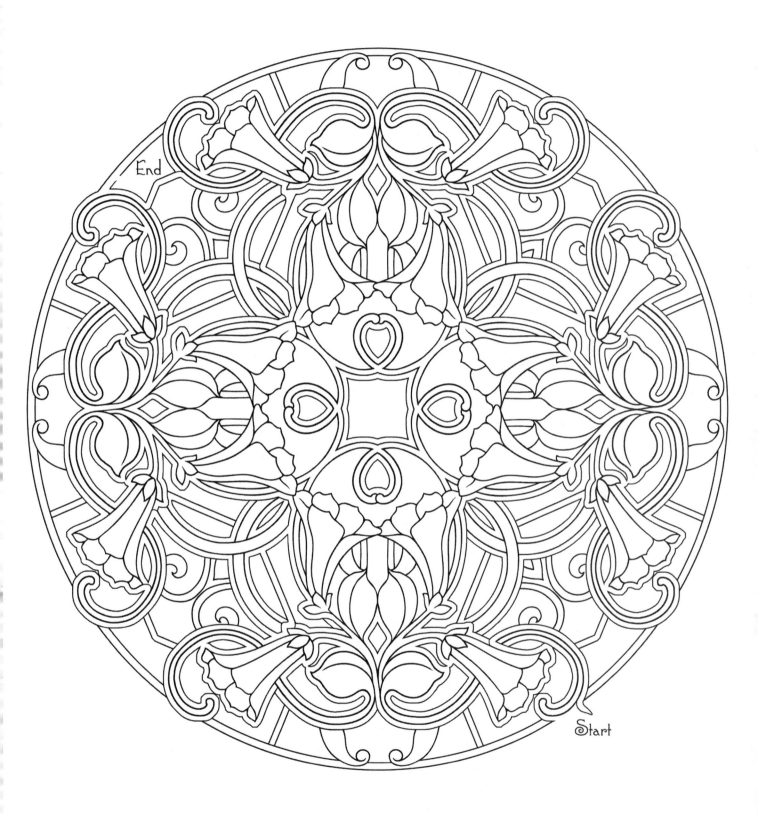

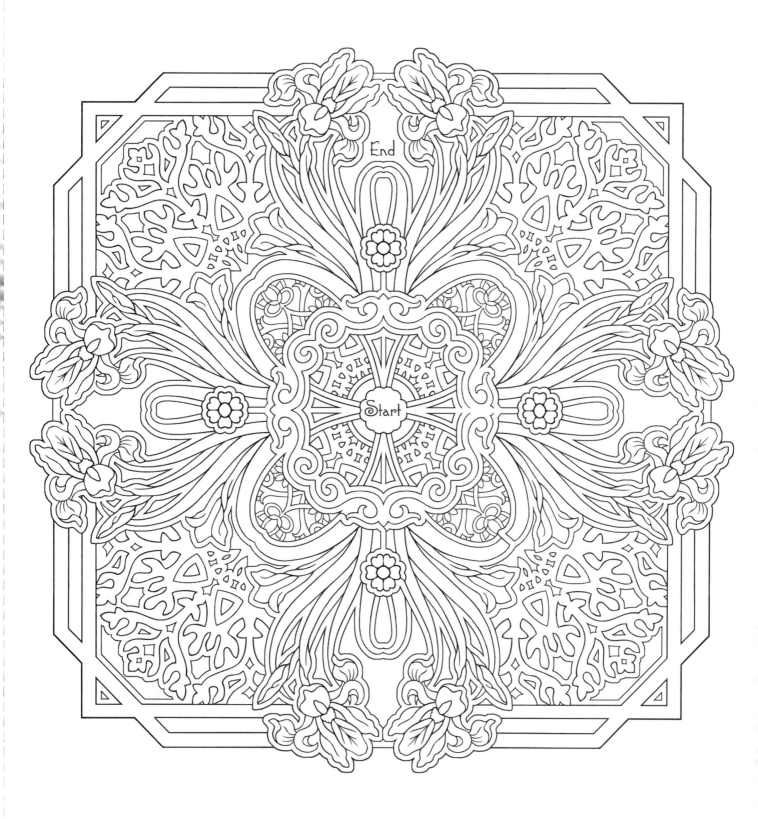

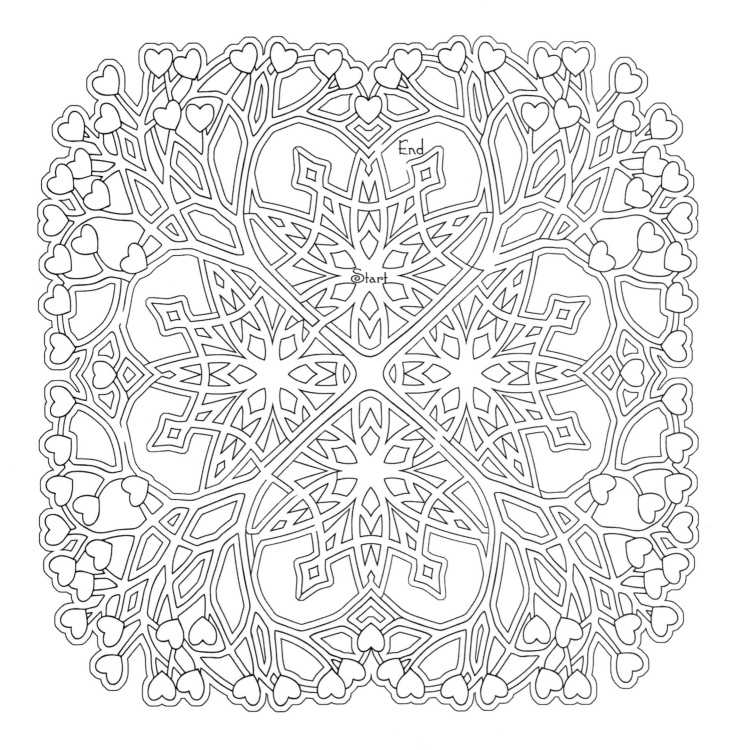

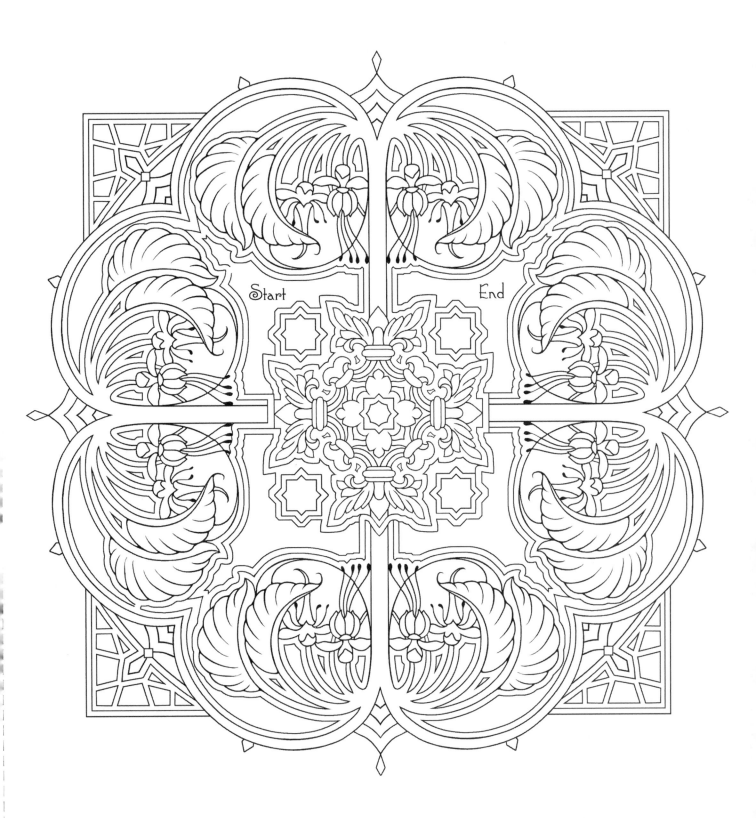
Start

End

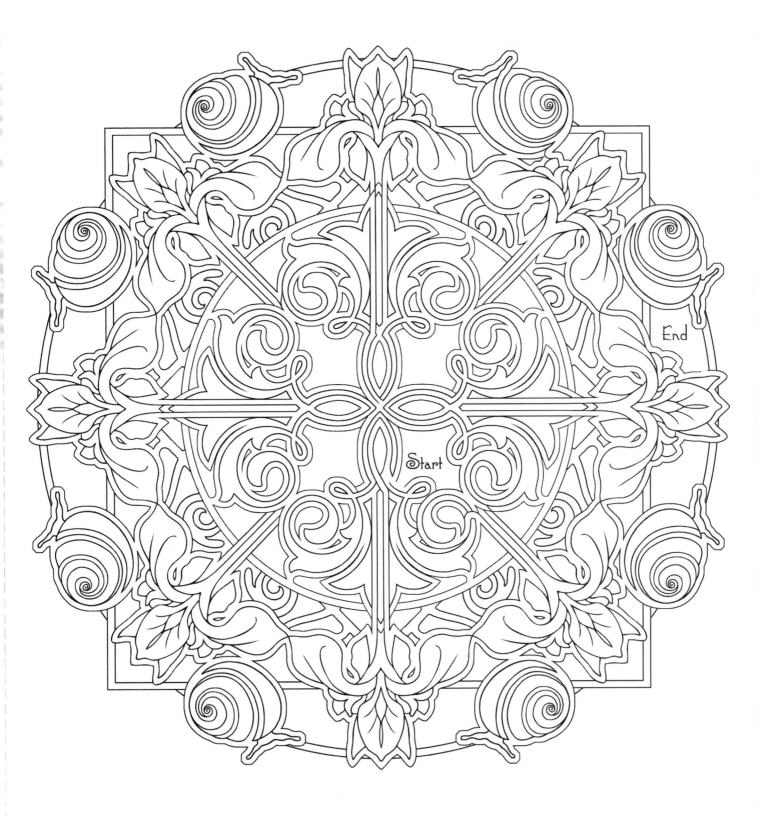

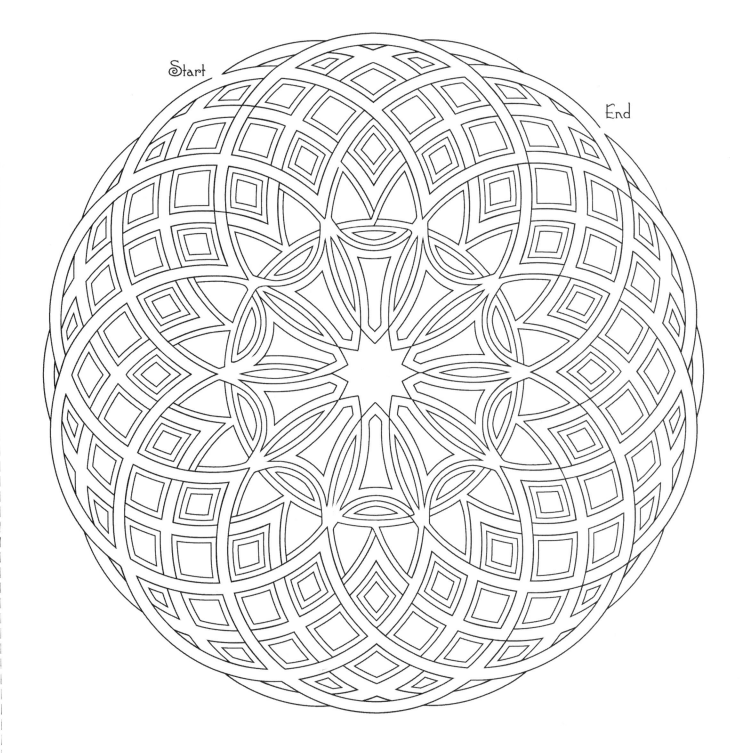

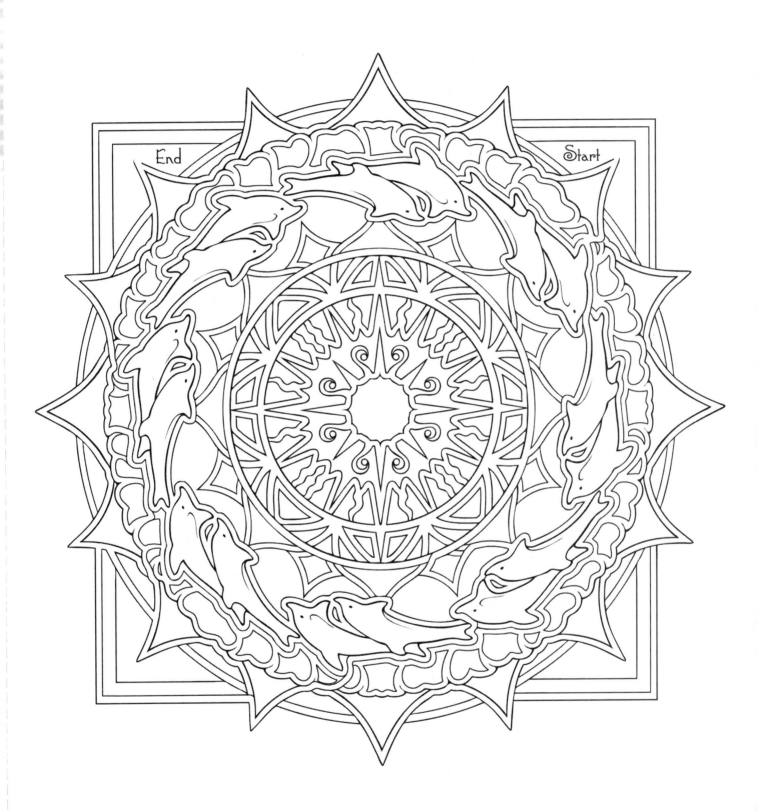
End

Start

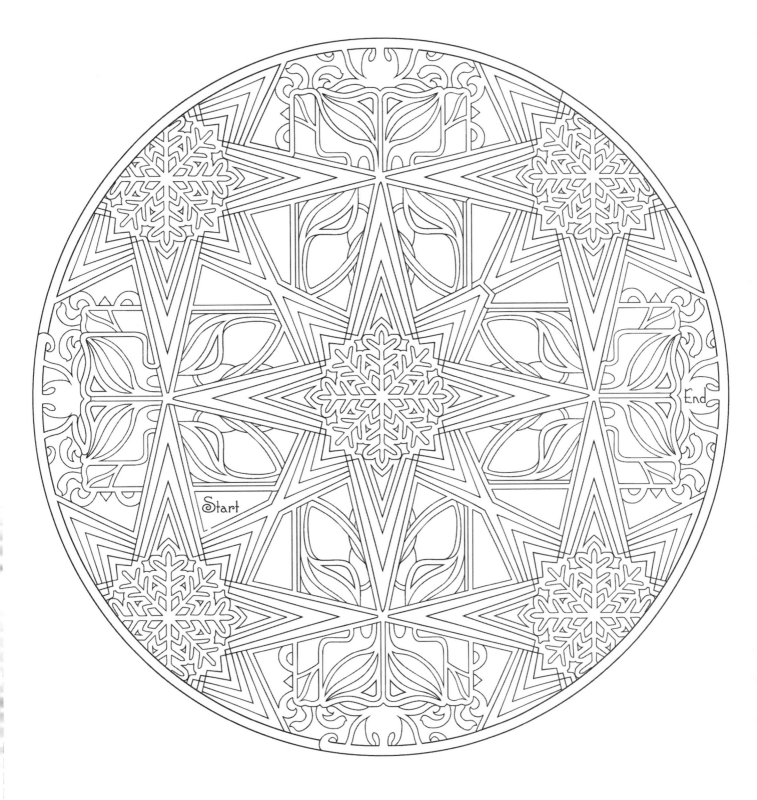

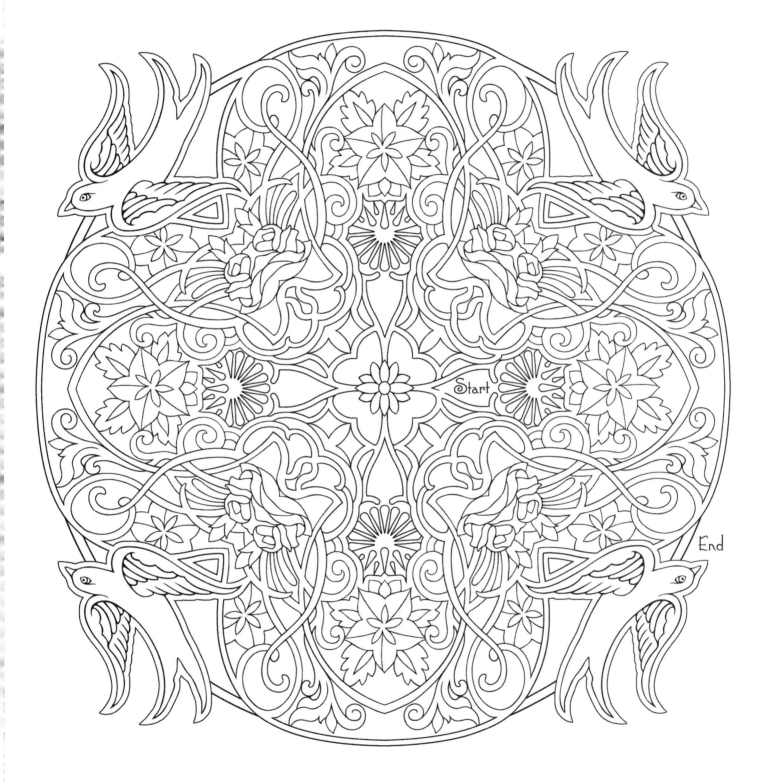

maze answer key

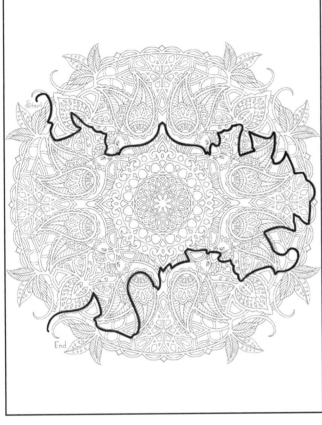

1

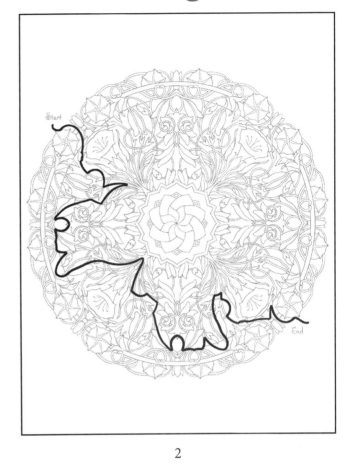

2

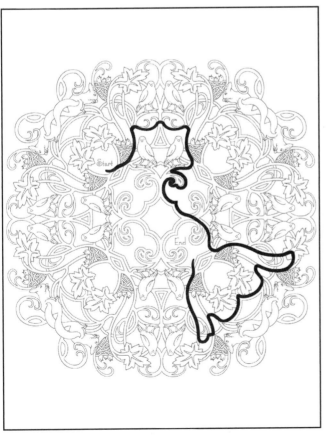

3

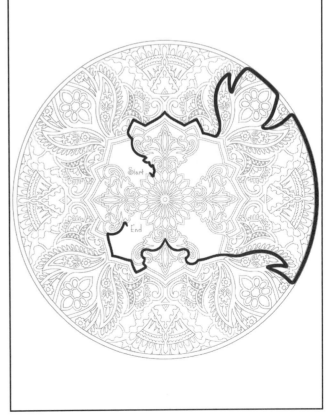

4

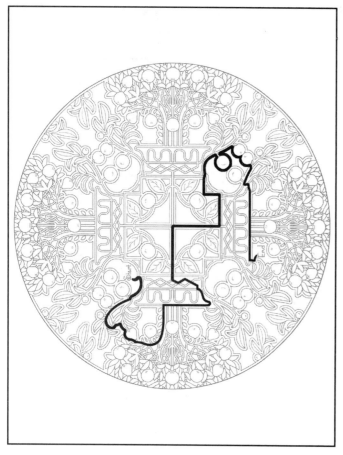

5

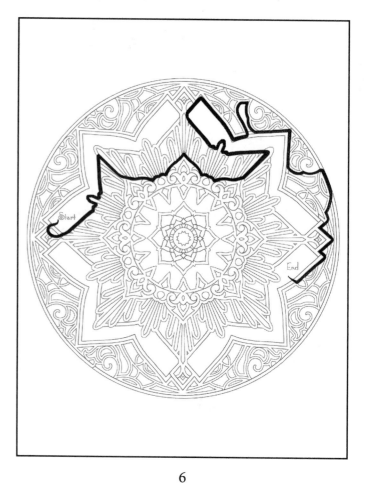

6

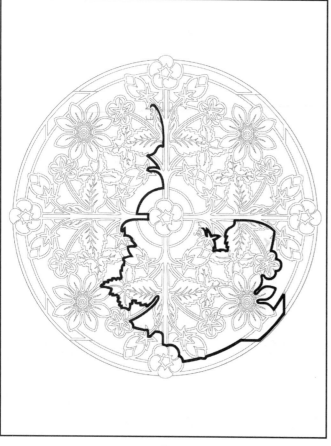

7

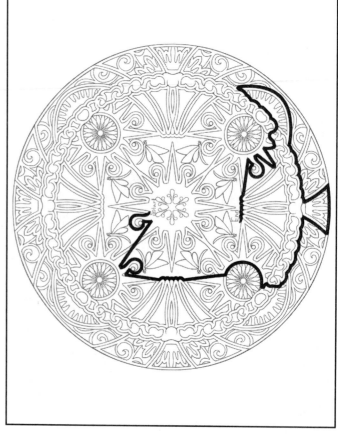

8

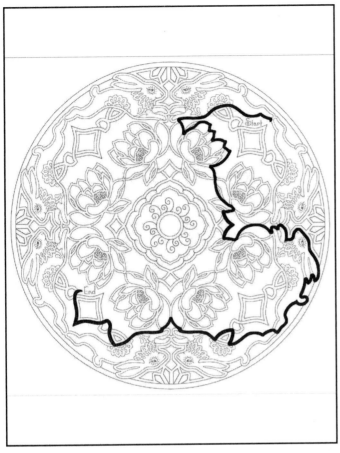

9

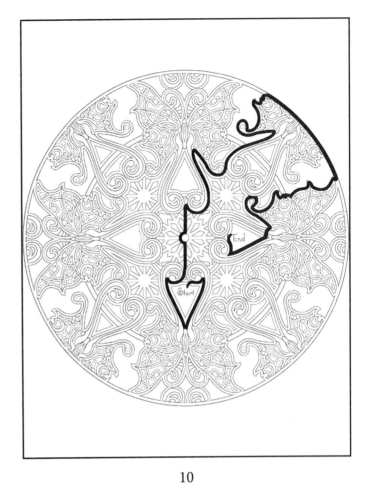

10

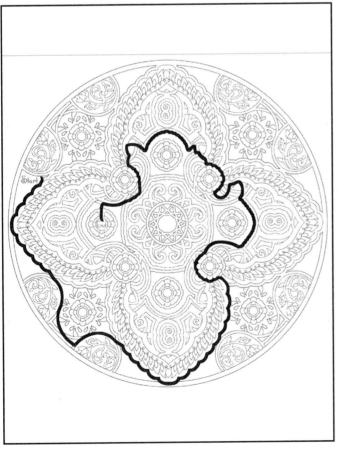

11

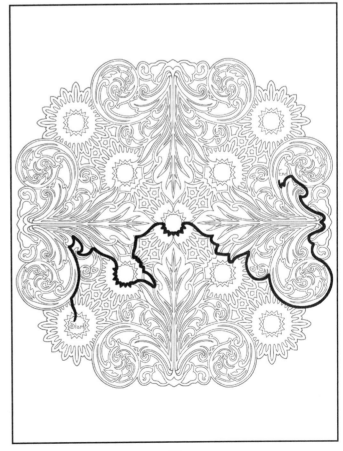

12

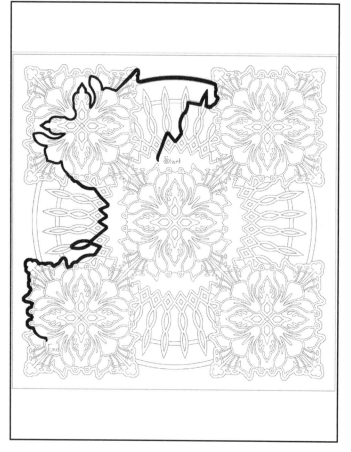

13

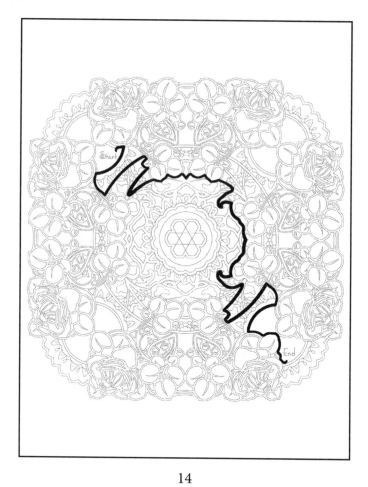

14

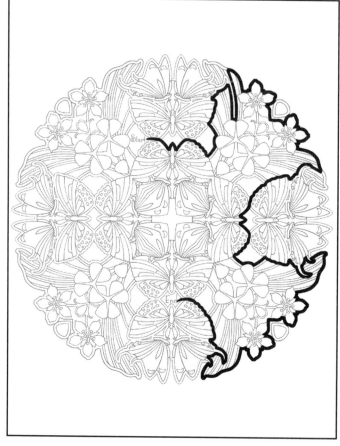

15

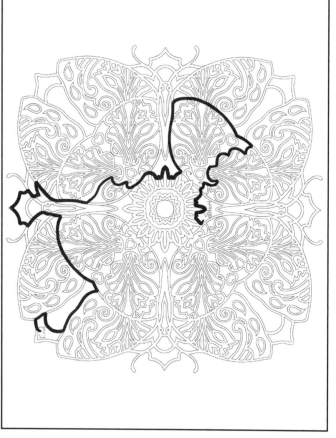

16

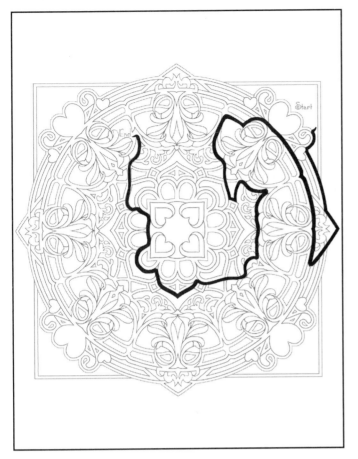

17

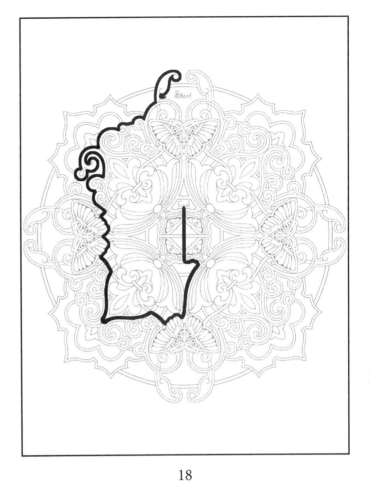

18

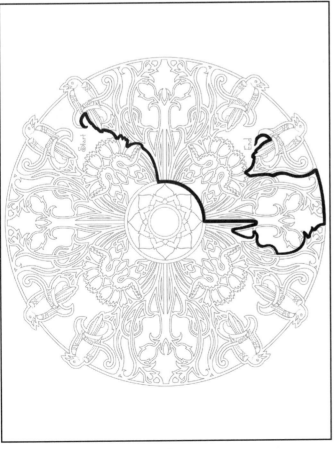

19

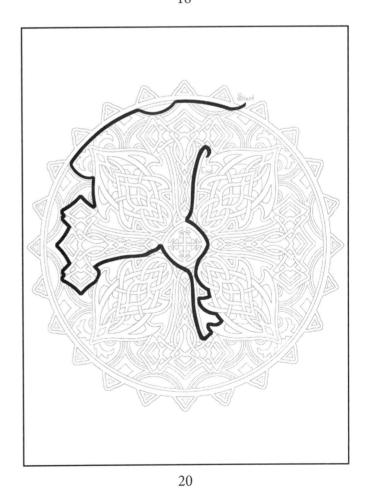

20

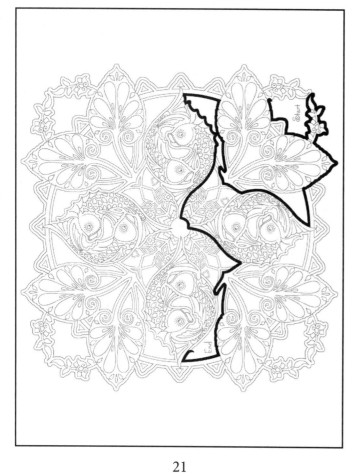

21

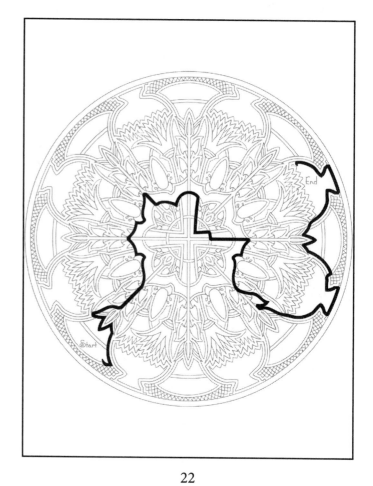

22

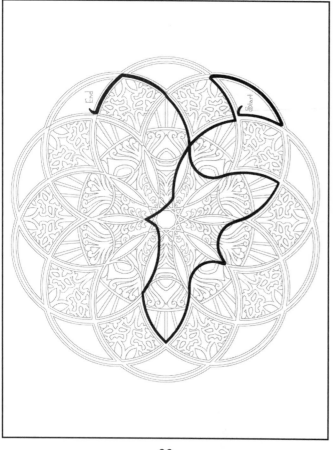

23

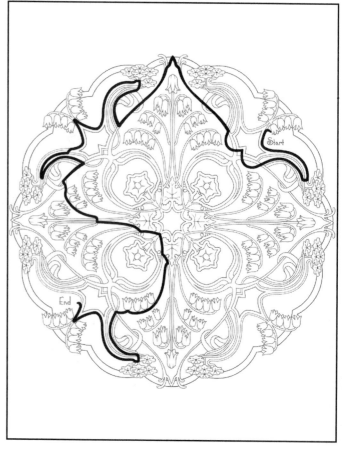

24

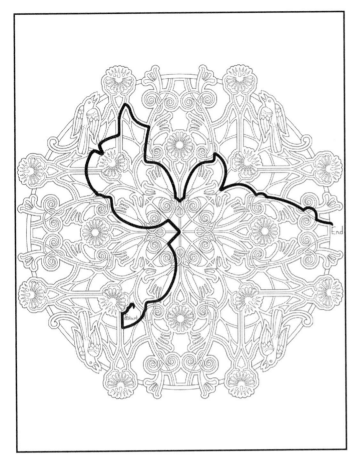

25

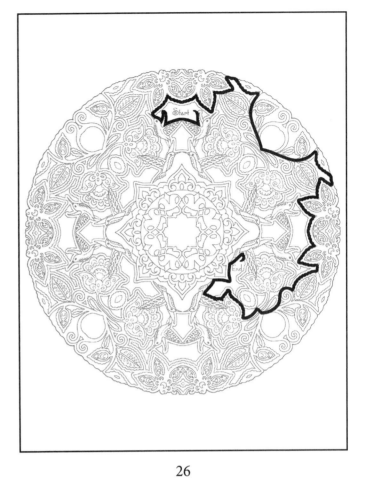

26

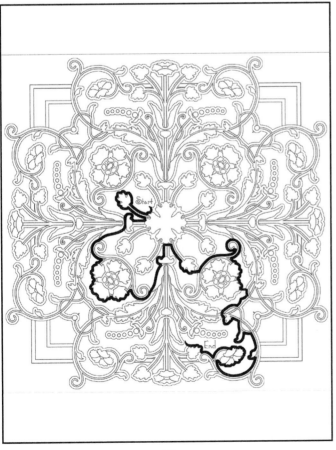

27

28

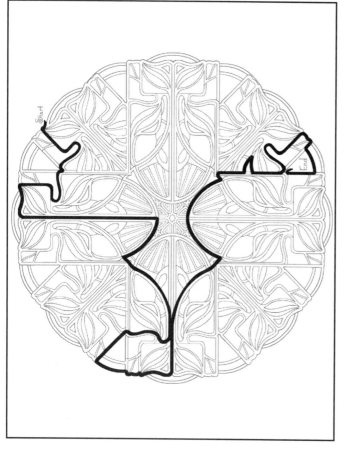

29

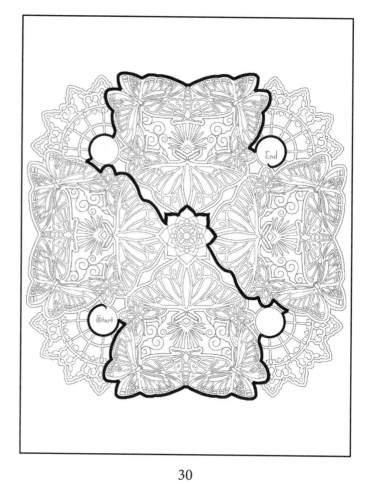

30

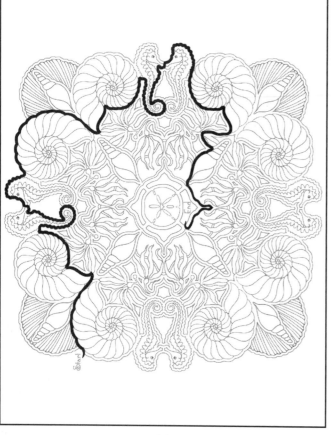

31

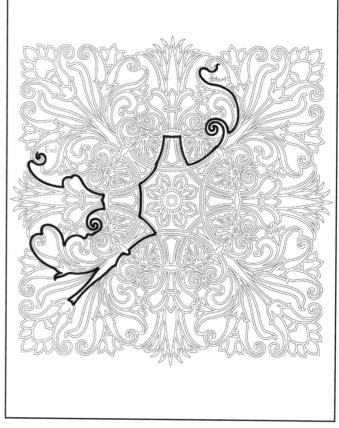

32

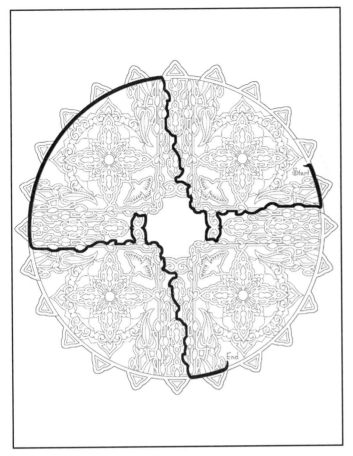

33

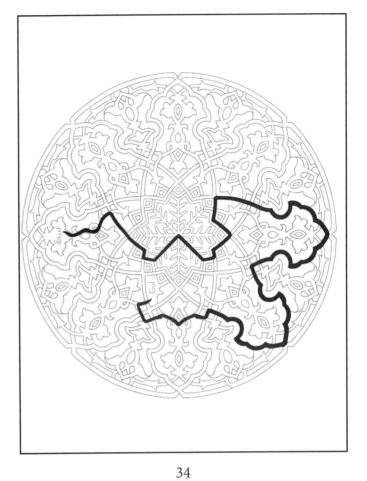

34

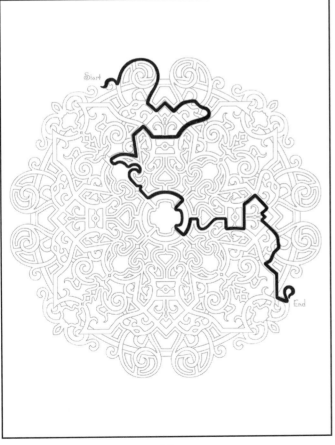

35

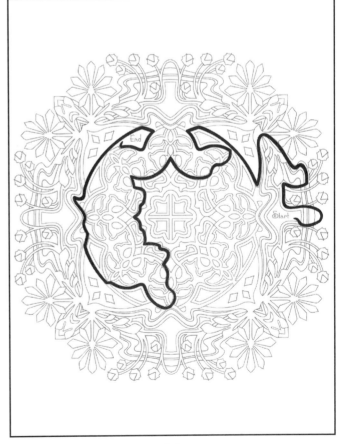

36

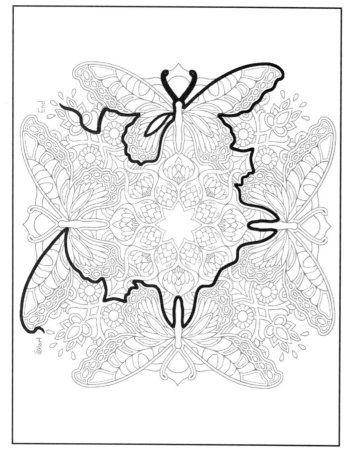

37

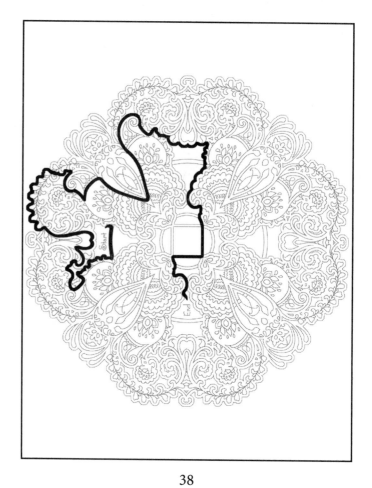

38

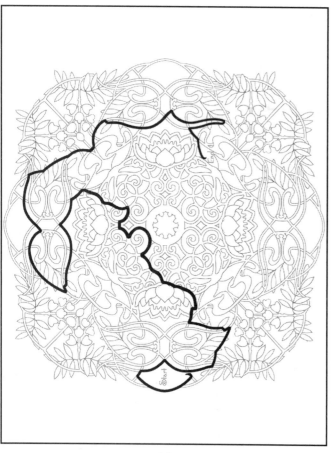

39

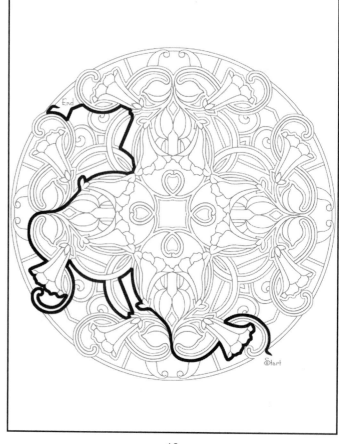

40

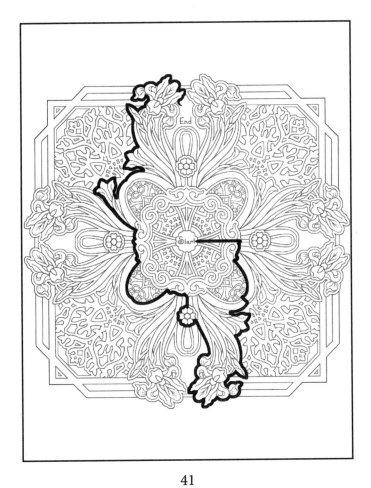

41

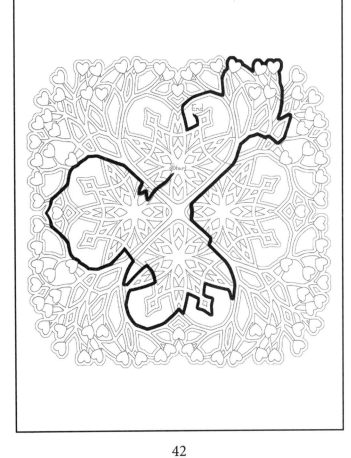

42

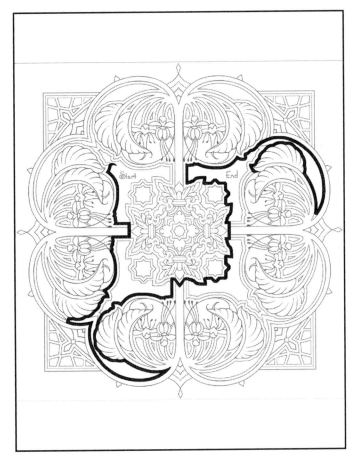

43

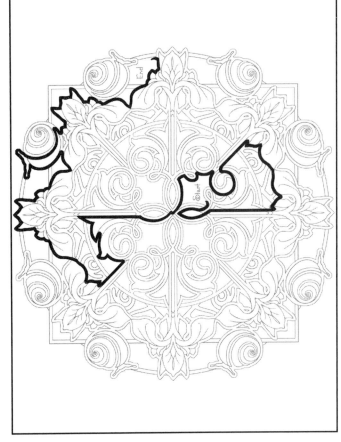

44

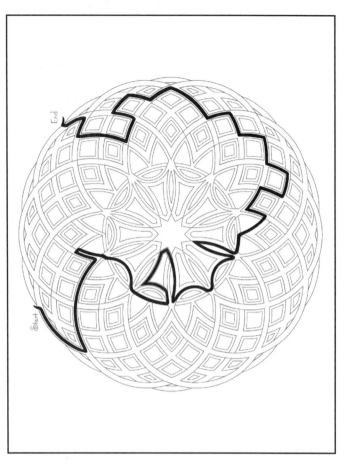

45

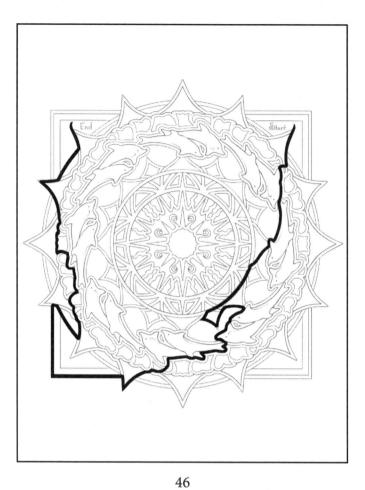

46

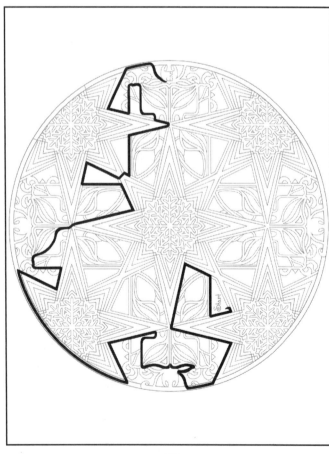

47

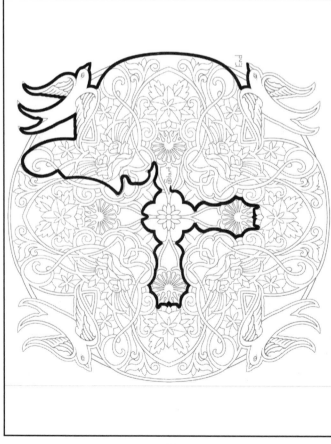

48